*W*atching
*B*irds

Reflections
on
the
Wing

Ann Taylor

AN AUTHORS GUILD BACKINPRINT.COM EDITION

Watching Birds
Reflections on the Wing
All Rights Reserved © 2000, 2003 by Ann Taylor

AN AUTHORS GUILD BACKINPRINT.COM EDITION

Published by iUniverse, Inc.

For information address:
iUniverse
2021 Pine Lake Road, Suite 100
Lincoln, NE 68512
www.iuniverse.com

Originally published by Ragged Mountain Press

Acknowledgments for previously published material appear on pages 161–62,
which constitute an extension of the copyright page

ISBN: 0-595-29115-5

Printed in the United States of America

For my mother,
who taught me to keep my eyes open
and who still doesn't miss a thing

The most precious things in life are near at hand,
without money and without price.
Each of you has the whole wealth of the
universe at your very door.
All that I ever had, or still have,
may be yours by stretching forth
your hand and taking it.

John Burroughs

Contents

Introduction

I'm grateful that the birds in my life never complain about a grade, nor do they expect me to drive them to migration. Unlike my students and my family, they occupy a special niche where I have no commitments unless I choose to make them. I am never called on to referee their differences of opinion, and I have nothing at all to teach them. Where birds are concerned, I am always the amateur, always the learner.

Since all too recently embarrassing myself at an Audubon Sanctuary bird feeder, where I carefully traced out the field marks of my first black-capped chickadee—my own state bird—I have never since been totally unaware of the birds, no matter how busy I've been. That chickadee forced me to notice what I was missing. Driving to school, I almost land in the ditch as I try to trace a kettle of hawks spiraling over the highway. At a faculty meeting, I cringe when I discover that a migrating Blackburnian warbler has just crashed into the high window and broken its neck. During lulls in my son's soccer game, I watch a noisier competition between a kingbird and an invading crow.

Too often, all I have time for are these glimpses out of the corner of my eye, but like the natural historian John Burroughs, who described a flock of swans winging over his cabin as "a breeze in my mind, like a noble passage in a poem," I too am inspired by birds. I am refreshed by their presence, even if only in passing. I look for them when I'm traveling, and I read about them whenever I can steal time. Exploring my own books or the more professional *Wilson Library Bulletin, Auk,* or *Condor* at the library is almost as much fun as my childhood reading of Jane Austen by the streetlamp outside my bedroom window when I was supposed to be asleep. It's true that titles enticing to the experts—"Temporal Dynamics of Neotropical Birds with Special Reference to Frugivores in Second-Growth Woods"—may calm the breezes of inspiration for me, but others—"Secrets of the Swift," "Winter of the Bobolink," "Prothonotary and Kentucky Warblers on Cozumel Island, Quintana Roo, Mexico"—can set them blowing again.

I also enjoy writing about the birds, yet another way for me to escape the business of my life. When the stack of uncorrected student papers seems to replenish itself no matter how many I read, pushed automatically from the bottom like cafeteria saucers, or when the saucers in my kitchen outstack the compositions, I sometimes escape to my own writing and try to capture fleeting moments with the birds. With words, I try to make sense of the birds in the field, the birds in the books, and the birds in my head.

This book is a record of those escapes—reflecting not the systematic learning of the scholar but the serendipitous discoveries of the devoted amateur—the many ways of watching the birds, the recognition of meanings both sought and unsought, the sharing of larger rhythms, and the compulsion to ask larger questions. Some of the encounters are immediate and personal, others at great distances from home, and still others in the vaster time and grander geography that only books and imagination allow.

Ways of Watching

Watching the Watchers

I'm at Italy's Lake Avernus, the "birdless" lake of ancient mythology, the poisonous entrance to the Underworld, and I'm looking for a particular bird—like the one I photographed many years ago.

Annually afflicted with watching my slides of Roman literary sites, my classics students always declare my bird to be a speck of dust on the film, but I know it's a bird. Because of Avernus's toxic reputation, I remember my surprise the first time I saw one flying there, and I remember snapping the picture. Because it was way beyond my talents as a bird-watcher, I never knew its name, but I placed it with confidence among the small-speck species. So I'm here to make another, more convincing slide, maybe of a bird I can name.

I think it was literature that nudged me into watching birds in the first place, not only this speck of a bird at Virgil's Avernus, but other literary birds—troubadours' and minnesingers' birds, Dante's and Chaucer's, Keats's and Shelley's. Maybe it was Poe's raven that got to me first, the one that quoth "Nevermore" again and again through my school years, or maybe it was T. S. Eliot's catalog of birds at nearby Cape Ann, the ones that stirred him to proclaim, somewhat ravenously, "All are delectable."

Maybe it's too many survey courses, taken and taught. But I do know that birds remind me of literature and literature reminds me of birds. They seem to occupy the same habitat in my mind, and they often fly in one another's company.

At Mount Auburn Cemetery, a bird landing spot in Cambridge, Massachusetts, I listen carefully to the fading melody of an ovenbird and finally come up with its name. Almost immediately, Robert Frost's lines about that bird's song come to mind:

> *The question that he frames in all but words*
> *Is what to make of a diminished thing.*

The bird's song is just a song to me, a pretty, drifting melody, an identifying field mark; Frost's words translate that song into metaphor and draw me into thoughts about loneliness and loss—sort of an *explication de chant*.

I recall no particular book or bird, no special spark of recognition that flamed into an urge to buy binoculars and a field guide and set out in hot pursuit, but I can recall a growing curiosity while reading comments like those in *Walden* where Thoreau tracks the devious tricks of a loon, "It was a pretty game, played on the smooth surface of the pond, a man against a loon," or where he listens to the owl's "Hoo hoo hoo, hoorer hoo" and exclaims with characteristic directness, "I rejoice that there are owls."

When I put down my books, I love discovering the brave birds at Avernus, the spring migrants in England, the songsters at Mount Auburn, the laughing loons at Walden. When I lower my

binoculars, I love recalling what the writers s
flying through my life.

Without any literary impetus, I identit   , first black-
capped chickadee and heard clearly its famous *chick-a-dee-dee-dee*
song at an Audubon Sanctuary where I stalked it as if it were on
the endangered species list. This bird no doubt had fluttered
around my head during all my years in Massachusetts, but I had
never really noticed it. I wouldn't call it an "epiphany" chickadee,
but thereafter the multitudinous chickadee references that I had
previously missed in literature (in much the same way I had missed
the birds themselves in my own backyard) took on new meaning.

"Think we should all get to work on our life lists?" asked one
bemused student working on his M.A. in English. "Of course!" I
replied, "I don't think that'd be a bad idea at all . . . and by the way,
what's the Massachusetts state bird?"

Over the years I came to understand other reasons for turning to bird-watching—almost as many reasons as there are watchers. Devotees describe it variously in written accounts: a sport, a
game of recognition, a satisfaction of the hunting and collecting
instincts. They may see it as freedom from the artificiality and gad-
getry of the man-made, a "ventilation of the psyche," or an oppor-
tunity to monitor the environment with "ecological litmus paper."
The more mystical may take it as a pursuit of tranquillity, of mys-
tery, of enlightenment, as a "quickening of our loftiest impulses."

In a much-quoted passage, James Fisher summarizes some of
the ways you can look at bird-watching:

> *The observation of birds may be a superstition, a tradition, an art,*
> *a science, a pleasure, a hobby, or a bore; this depends entirely on the*
> *nature of the observer.*

Joseph Hickey offers a humorous perspective:

> *By some, it is regarded as a mild paralysis of the central nervous system, which can be cured only by rising at dawn and sitting in a bog. Others regard it as a harmless occupation of children, into which maiden aunts may sometimes relapse.*

Now that my own motivation has moved beyond literary annotation, I'm not sure where I would place myself among these many types (although I haven't headed for a bog at dawn). But I am sure I could place many other watchers I have met in the field. I have yet to flush out the cliché bird-watcher of popular misconception—that knobby-kneed simpleton in pith helmet, striped shirt, baggy plaid shorts, argyle socks, and lumpy shoes—a type of eccentric loony. My discoveries have been real people, not cartoons—some bored, some frustrated, some pretentious, some even cranky, but all worthy of a place in my life list of bird-watchers.

I think of the elderly gentleman in a three-piece tweed suit, hustling out of his Mercedes with Illinois plates at Newburyport Harbor in Massachusetts to see a Ross's gull, a rarity blown in from the far north. Using his cane like an oar, he stroked himself over a muddy tire track. "Is he still here?" he asked breathlessly.

"Right over there, by the boat," I replied, happy that I had scouted the boatyard first and feeling a certain pressure to hurry for both of them. The Ancient Mariner came to mind.

I think also of the woman in her sixties, "an old schoolmarm," she said, sitting alone on a low deck of an Atlantic-tossed boat. Without binoculars or bird books, she held tight to the slippery rail as the boat lurched over the waves. Water poured relentlessly from the hood of her red cape down to the toes of her L.L. Bean boots. "I'm waiting for a parasitic jaeger," she reported with equanimity, as if she were expecting a pupil to drop in for extra tutoring after school. Getting off the boat, she signaled me a thumbs-up.

I think too of the watchers at Mount Wachusett, where every October thousands of hawks migrate down the central Massachusetts stretch of the Eastern Flyway, riding the thermals with wings stretched stiff. The hilltop is prickly with telescopes focused long distance in all directions. The mood is relaxed, expectant; that is, until the call in front of me, "Kettle of sharpies at two o'clock!" or behind me, "Redtail coasting left of tower . . . above the horizon!" sends everyone scurrying.

I turn one way, then the other, hoping to see something more than sky, clouds, and what look like large congregations of fleas. I'm not even sure what a kettle is. Here I must trust the regulars, those who follow the count for days on end, who keep the chalkboard records up to the minute, and who know their hawks. By the time I find a hawk and then decide if its shins are sharp or not, it'll be sunning in South America. So I turn first to the watchers with the HAWK and RAPTOR license plates on their pickup trucks and follow their directions as the birds rise in chaotic spirals way, way above my head.

I've met other enthusiasts, those keeping not only life lists but year, country, state, day, trip, yard, and back steps lists, the ones with the birdy t-shirts: "Think well of the crane!" or "Visit Hawk Mountain: Where It Counts!" (Antismoking bird-watchers seem drawn to swaggering puffins, butts drooping from their beaks: "Stop Puffin'!" says the shirt.) These full-time watchers may well drift off to sleep conjuring up lists of 700 birds for a

North American year, or tallying all 8,600-plus species world-wide.

On a pelagic trip to Stellwagen Bank off the Boston coast, I watched a group of this type take a humpback whale in stride, get mildly stirred by the schoolmarm's jaeger, and merely glance at a shearwater. But they changed their tune when a Sabine's gull emerged from a flock of unremarkables.

"A Sabine's!" yelled one. "I can't believe it!" She rummaged her checklist out of her backpack.

"I thought it was, but I didn't dare call," shouted another. "I was afraid you'd all think I was nuts!"

Their excitement was contagious, and I soon found myself lurching from rail to rail with them, keeping the Sabine's in sight. Not knowing a Sabine's from a sparrow before this trip, I joined in the high fives and added this bird to my own list, with an exclamation point. On the way home I couldn't help thinking of the lonely Anglo-Saxon "Wanderer," exiled at sea with only memories of his beloved land companions and with a touch of envy for the birds themselves, conspicuously in groups:

> *Then from his sleep he wakes—the friendless man—,*
> *Seeing before him gray waves,*
> *Sea-birds bathing, with feathers outspread.*

Thinking of him, I appreciated even more having shared my bird with these old salts of the seabird set.

Among the many birders on my list, no one seemed more taken with the birds than a certain spring warbler–watcher on Massachusetts's Marblehead Neck. As I approached him in a small, deserted clearing, he didn't lower his binoculars, didn't even murmur a hello.

Looking more like a Wrestlemania contestant than a birdwatcher, his binoculars almost hidden in one huge hand, he focused on a young birch. "There are days you'd kill for a Wilson's!" he declared abruptly, causing me to estimate how far behind me on the trail my husband was. My literary mind drifted not to warbler poems but to Stephen King.

"Now take a look at that!" he exclaimed, "Must be fifteen in one tree!" Not even sure he was talking to me, I peered into the birch and saw a flurry deep in the greenery.

Shuffling softly toward the tree, he whispered, still without lowering his binoculars. "Would you believe? I had to take a day off from work last week 'cause everything that moved began to look like a warbler." He paused. "And now this! Never saw so many Wilson's!"

I tried to remember what a Wilson's was. Then, with my own binoculars, I made out some tiny yellow birds with olive green wings, lost among the leaves. "Must be the Wilson's," I thought, feeling too silly to ask.

He finally turned my way, binoculars lowered only slightly, ready for action. "By the way, did you see that elusive baybreasted on your way in here?" My answer, that I had seen only a "prominent Blackburnian," drew no response. He raised his binoculars again. I felt the way I used to when Sister Rita Bernadine's chilly silence rebuked some childish quip during religion class.

"Gotta get that bay-breasted," he finally sighed, turning and disappearing into the evergreen shadows.

Bird artist Lee Jacques once said, "The difference between a warbler and no warblers is very slight," but he hadn't met this guy. These devoted types give me courage to withstand the occasional "yellow-bellied sapsucker" joke or comments from English majors who wonder why I waste my time looking at skylarks at Merlin's Stonehenge or chickadees at Thoreau's Walden. Against such critics, the best watchers give me confidence; but when I'm in their company myself, all my confidence takes wing. I'm inspired by their enthusiasm but more often awed and intimidated by their quick identifications. My comma on the Atlantic horizon is their Manx shearwater. My five little birds in a tree are their parula, three yellows, and a redstart. I wouldn't call a bird in their presence if it sat still for a portrait in oils or pointed itself out personally in my field guide.

Probably because of this insecurity, I always enjoy E. B. White's comments on the autumn chestnut-sided warbler's lemony shade of green:

> Well, it is sufficient for recognition if you happen to be standing, or lying, directly under a Chestnut-sided Warbler in the fall of the year and can remember not to confuse the issue with "adults in spring" or with the Bay-breast at any season—especially the female Bay-breast in spring, which is rather dim and indistinct, the way all birds look to me when they are in a hurry (which they almost always are) or when I am.

Considering how often I share White's sentiments, particularly trying to name those little avian no-see-ums, I doubt I'll ever make it through Peterson's three stages: looker, lister, and finally full-fledged watcher. I have no list beyond a spotty life list; I've never had a Big Day or even a Small one, nor have I memorized the chirps, squawks, twitters, thumps, and trills on the Cornell Laboratory's birdsong tapes.

I've never studied bird skins or recorded courtship habits. I've never graduated to ecology, bird censuses, banding techniques, or conservation programs. Nor have I fallen from a cliff, been attacked by a tawny owl or a lammergeier, or been chased by bandits, bulls, whales, or a flock of frantic flamingos—all documented as telltale markings of the full-fledged bird-watcher.

I have, however, sat in a classroom patting a stuffed dovekie rocking on its platform, and I've trailed through eel grass on marshy Monomoy Island looking for a bald eagle affectionately named "E 11." I've crawled over craggy boulders for a close-up photograph of a feeding puffin, my bird masterpiece, a sunlit calendar puffin with its yellow beak firmly clamped on a school of little silver fish.

I've also stood in snowy woods while my tape recorder conversed with a barred owl, and I've held the feathery vitality of an ovenbird while it was being banded, then felt the peculiar thrill of releasing it to a nearby maple where it indignantly puffed itself up. Saint Francis came to mind. And then there was his poem . . . the one about Brother Sun and Sister Moon.

I've also sat content for nearly two hours while two male mallards competed with much splashing for a choice nesting site and a coy female. Our guide kept repeating, "Now *there's* some behavior." I'm also on my second copy of *A Field Guide to the Birds*, autographed by Roger Tory Peterson at his Boston Public Library lecture on penguins.

The more I have experiences like these, the more real birds I see, the more my literary birds come to life. Now that I've heard ravens in person, Poe's bird saying "Nevermore!" will forever sound like the gravelly gabber he really is. I can now see and hear that laughing loon playing its "pretty game" with Thoreau on the pond.

Reading Henry Beston's *Outermost House*, about his year alone on Cape Cod, I've always loved his famous bird passage:

> *In a world older and more complete than ours they move finished and complete, gifted with extensions of the senses we have lost or never attained, living by voices we shall never hear. They are not our brethren, they are other nations, caught with ourselves in the net of life and time, fellow prisoners of the splendour and travail of the earth.*

But it took my own time with the birds to help me understand Beston's big picture, his own personal journey from the sand, the shells, the froth, and the feathers on the beach to speculations about the nature of life itself. Even Wallace Stevens's elusive "Thirteen Ways of Looking at a Blackbird" makes greater sense to me now, particularly this stanza:

> *I do not know which to prefer,*
> *The beauty of inflections*
> *Or the beauty of innuendoes,*
> *The blackbird whistling*
> *Or just after.*

I can now hear better the subtle connection he is making between poetry and the rhythms of birdsong, between the songs and the silences, and I enjoy even more both the poem and the bird.

Here at Lake Avernus, twenty birds—some of them kittiwakes for sure—are flying high above the ancient crater, and I have an indisputable slide for the next wave of classics students. I have twenty identified proofs that Virgil's vaporous Avernus is now frequented by living birds. This literary site is no longer birdless. Like so much literature, it is alive with birdsong.

A Blessing for a Lifetime

The great gray owl silently hunkered down in the cornfield, only six feet away from me and a small circle of watchers, mostly families. In spite of this attention and whispered comments from parents to children, this wide-eyed rarity from the winter north stayed still except for occasionally puffing up his slaty feathers. On the ground, eager photographers eased even closer, inch by inch, as if on low-fire maneuvers. I glanced down at my son, then seven months old, busy trying to eat the prickly stubble as he sat beside me, ignoring the owl.

Bored, Geoff squealed, cutting through the respectful hush. At the same moment the owl flapped his wings high, dipped his head, and opened the yellow disks of his eyes even wider. He focused full attention on what might have been an oversized, boisterous mouse; Geoff, himself wide-eyed, stared back. I bent quickly to pick him up, and at the same instant I noticed that the baby and the owl, still staring, seemed stopped in time, bound in a private alliance.

On the "as the tot is bent" theory, I had already stocked up on toys with an ecological aura—a park ranger truck, rubber spiders, snakes, and frogs, woodland coloring books, ocean posters, and a stuffed duck, and I had already hung bird mobiles from the ceiling of the nursery. Add to this the bird feeder near the high chair at the kitchen window and the nightly exploration of the *My First Birds* pop-up book, and it isn't really surprising that I was more than ready to take that moment between bird and baby as symbolic. The owl may have been sizing him up for supper, but I couldn't resist transforming that glare into a sort of ocular blessing, a private summoning to the company of birds and their watchers.

Latecomers to the field, my husband and I were determined that Geoff would share this part of our lives, perhaps to move early beyond our forever amateur skills, so I immediately assumed the owl's good wishes.

The following summer I wheeled Geoff's carriage to the unlovely remains of the extinct dodo encased at Oxford's Museum of Natural History, then showed him the big archaeopteryx drawings. In Boston I daily pointed out the cormorants balancing on the Charles River buoys; then he started pointing them out to me. Over those early years, he inherited out-of-focus binoculars from my father's abandoned auction treasures and, even without them, became skilled at spotting robins and cardinals, the cardinal by song as well as sight. I was convinced that he was living up to what that owl had in mind for him.

But I must admit that, endowed as he was, he seemed to have other ideas for himself. In the years that followed, he came to prefer his bulldozer and army jeep to his ranger truck, and his favorite book, ragged and taped from overuse, was not *My First Birds* but *Big Work Machines*, with lines like, "In the forest, trees are cut down to be made into lumber for furniture and houses" or

"Hundreds of workers digging with hand shovels could not dig a big hole as fast as an excavator can." He always caught me when I tried to ease by the totally birdless logging machines page, and he studied the "metal arms," "sharp blades," and "deeply treaded tires" with even greater affection. As we drove along the river, he became much more likely to name the scrapers, graders, and front-end loaders reshaping the riverbank than to bother with the cormorants. About that time I devoted one Christmas shopping season to finding just the right cherry picker truck, the one with the big wheels, rotating arm, and adjustable bucket.

I did sometimes wonder if he would ever want the seat at the Bird-watchers' Round Table where I was holding him a reservation. In this land of tough cops and temperamental terminators, I wondered if this lover of tall steel cranes would ever appreciate the feathered ones. Then there were the times when I wondered if I wanted him to.

Bird-watchers are, after all, too often subjects for humor, even mockery. The bird-watcher of popular mythology is middle-aged to elderly, overweight or scrawny, and always silly. The men are silly looking with pith helmets and baggy shorts. The women wear silly-looking combat boots and granny glasses. Descendants of the impractical medieval scholars, so taken by higher thoughts that they fall into any handy pit, bird-watchers are often portrayed as bumblers. They trek awkwardly through swamp and brier patch, trip over twigs, fall out of trees—while the sniggering and elusive birds look on with amusement or make nests on their heads.

In cartoons, bird-watchers say things like "No, no, think of the quail" or "Hark! I hear a woodcock on the wing!" Or they look insane, as in the old flower delivery advertisement where the courier dashes past the dotty bird-watcher sinking obliviously into quicksand. In a cartoon showing a theatrical agency waiting room, the receptionist asks, "Which one of you does the bird imitations?" Needless to say, the birdy applicant is the one flapping around the room, above the heads of the more firmly grounded weight lifter, ventriloquist, and viola player.

They are also subjects for mocking toleration and sometimes annoyance. One woman writes sadly of her husband's birdwatching habit, seeing it as an incurable ailment and responding to his most enthusiastic sightings as if she were "strangling on hot porridge," the way some of my students respond to my own weekend victories. And recently, while I was snooping out an oriole's nest suspended above a public parking lot, a group of teenagers in a convertible chirped and twittered every time I lifted my binoculars. When I smiled and pointed out the nest, they rolled their eyes and snickered.

Sometimes even the birds get annoyed, as in a playful magazine sketch of a tattered "overwatched bird," eyes glazed and tail feathers drooping—a victim of bird paparazzi. An old Bermuda ordinance goes so far as to promise rectification of birds' grievances: "From now on, they are going to get as much consideration, on a smaller scale, as the tourists."

It isn't always easy to be a bird-watcher, though I do read encouraging news of increasing interest. Bird society memberships are on the rise, more volunteers join the Christmas Bird Counts, and there seems to be more concern for the environment in which birds play a vital part. Others claim that bird-watching is now an "in" sport. Says one hopeful apologist, "There was a time not too many years ago when looking at birds was considered odd by a large segment of the American public—not any more!" Encouraging.

I have also read a spirited defense of bird-watchers claiming that "some of the best bird-watchers in the country are former athletes who are also some of the most rugged outdoorsmen you ever saw." I'm sure that given their penchant for long walks and difficult searches, most bird-watchers probably *are* in good shape, but these "real men do bird-watch" arguments seem to overstate the athleticism involved. I still find it hard to imagine mud wrestlers or X-game sports fans devoting their springs to the warbler wave, but I hope I'm wrong.

It seems that, for whatever reasons—fear of effeminacy, devotion to getting and spending, preference for brawn over brain, simple ignorance—bird-watching will probably continue as a target for undeserved humor.

What then am I still hoping for Geoff, now in his girl-watching teens, now likely to snicker along with those kids in the convertible? What am I hoping the owl was able to pass on to him that distant afternoon?

At the very least, I want Geoff to go on noticing the birds flying by, as he did on the highway last week when he spotted a turkey vulture high above the sunroof, or as he did today when, just outside the barbershop, he pointed out to all of us a flock of over two hundred starlings lining up neatly and noisily along the telephone wires.

And less daftly than in my dodo days, I still hope for more. I still have hopes that he will share the delight of writers like Thoreau, who see in nature the chance to respect something bigger than ourselves, the chance to hike a path, "however solitary and narrow and crooked," with "love and reverence." I want him to be attuned to the "higher and finer mood" of people like John Burroughs and to share in the promised "communication with our own souls" that comes as a reward, ironically, for looking with attention outside ourselves.

I still hope for him to fly with the eagles, skylarks, blackbirds, and owls winging through the long history of literature, and I want him to trace the intricate images of the artists—the classical, colorful lines of Audubon, the subtle shadings of Fuertes. I want him to watch and to listen, to feel his own delight, maybe to pass it on in whatever way he can.

But even if he finally comes up with only a bird-watching hobby, defined by Aldo Leopold as "in large degree useless, inefficient, laborious or irrelevant," I'll be grateful to that owl, no matter what his real intentions might have been.

An Owl or Not an Owl?

In recent years I've become bold at pointing out chickadees, robins, or cardinals, but otherwise I'm cautious with my identifications. And for good reason. In my literature classes, I'll never confuse Ben Jonson with Sam Johnson, or Beowulf with Virginia. With birds, however, I'm capable of errors of all degrees.

Take shorebirds. As the resting flocks of tiny dunlins, phalaropes, sandpipers, and sanderlings dash off in unison over the waves at my approach, I follow them with binoculars, hoping to match them up with the telltale "buffy underparts," "stouter bills," and "significant streaks" in my guide. But unless I can sneak up on them (and anyone who's tried to sneak up on a dunlin knows about that), I often must settle for the generic "shorebirds."

I might be able to capture greater yellowlegs for my life list, primarily because their yellow legs are long and bright, but first they have to stand up straight beside the lesser yellowlegs, which look a lot like them, so I can pick out the tall ones.

I have the same problem with common and arctic terns, both of which I observed for an entire morning at a nesting site on

Maine's Machias Seal Island. I knew that the common tern's bill is orange red with a black tip and that the arctic tern's is red to the tip, but I could never be sure which tip I was watching at the time. All the bills looked red sometimes, all looked black-tipped sometimes. All terns looked like either common or arctic terns. To an ornithologist, I'm sure this confusion would be like my mixing up whether Jonson or Johnson wrote *Rasselas*.

And what of the thousands of warblers, trouble enough during spring migration when their colors and patterns are most obvious, but impossible when they become, even to Peterson, "confusing fall warblers"? If *he's* confused, I'm permanently perplexed.

At times I'm absolutely sure of a bird identification, but the bird has to be unique, impossible to take for any other. At Kenya's Lake Nakuru, my *Guide to East African Birds* in hand, I couldn't miss the huge marabou storks grimly sizing up the equally unmistakable, and evidently edible, flamingos. The long-billed curlew too was hard to mistake, because its bill looked like Father Time's scythe. And I would recognize the iridescent blue green sprightliness of the hoopoe every time I saw one, but just how often will I get a chance to show off this particular bit of expertise? Hoopoes don't live in the United States, so only once in my life, alone with my husband on a dusty African jeep track, have I had occasion to announce, "Look! There's a hoopoe!"

Very early in my days as a watcher, in a conversation with an old-time member of a local bird club, I mentioned that I had seen a great white heron at Cape Cod. "No, dear," he replied politely, "probably *not* a great white. They live in Florida. Do you think it could have been an American egret, also big and white?" I erased the heron from my life list until later, when I did see that great white bird at home among the mangrove roots of the Everglades and wrote it back in.

Generally, then, I'm cautious. But last semester on the college grounds, where my authority sometimes reigns, I abandoned my usual hesitancy. Maybe it was because I was on my way to a *Don Quixote* class, familiar with the book from years of teaching, confident in my notes and plans. Maybe it was the timing— 7:45 A.M. on Monday, after a long Sunday afternoon of birdwatching. Maybe it was the academic buildings, the library looming behind me.

Strolling down the sunlit sidewalk to class, I was absentmindedly scanning the sky when I spotted a huge gray shape perched high on a home TV antenna across the street. Nearsighted enough to speed-read the mite-sized print of the condensed *Oxford English Dictionary* without the magnifying glass but blurry blind at any distance beyond my desk, I couldn't be sure what I was seeing. I knew it wasn't all antenna, though, and decided it must be a bird—a big bird!

I shaded my eyes, squinted, and tilted my head to various angles. The Monday-morning scholars passed me by. Finally one stopped—a weathered-looking blond in hiking boots, jeans, plaid shirt, and sheepskin vest. "Hey! What're you seein'?"

"A hawk, I think, but I can't tell what kind," I answered, much too quickly. Pointing to the roof of the blue house, I said, "It's up there on that antenna."

"Hey, yeah, I see it!" she said, shading her eyes and squinting at the roof. "Hey! I think it just moved. Wonder if it's going to take off!"

"Maybe," I answered, gliding into my professorial tones, "but hawks can stay in one place for quite a long time."

"Oh wow! What a gift!" She clapped her hands, took another look and then said, "I don't think it's a hawk, though . . . I think it's an owl . . . you know . . . like the one at the Museum of Science."

"Spooky is a great horned owl," I informed her, beginning to make out tufts of feathers on the bird's head and detecting a slight turn on its perch, "but it's really unusual to see an owl this time of day, right out in the open like that. I think you're right, though. It's not a hawk."

Checking my watch, I muttered, "We'd better get to class."

"Yeah . . . and thanks," she replied. "Wow!"

"Wow is right," I thought to myself as I climbed the stairs to my fourth-floor classroom. On the way up, I didn't resist detouring to my friend Jay's office, where he was discussing writing with three students. I announced the great horned owl to them and pointed out how rare it is to see one like this in the daytime. "It's up there on the antenna, if you want to take a look."

Delighted to abandon their papers, they all peered around the tree outside the window and tried to spot my owl. I told them I had seen it move and then left the four of them still gaping as I hurried upstairs to my classroom. Pens ready, fifteen Classics of World Lit. students awaited discussion of a significant episode in *Don Quixote*, the one where he mistakes a windmill for the giant Briraeus, attacks it with his crooked spear, and gets himself and his horse smashed to smithereens.

"Look!" I said, and beckoned all of them to the window. "Come here! Look over at that roof, the blue house with the TV antenna. You'll see a great horned owl sitting there!"

Papers shuffled, books dropped, chairs grated on the floor as the entire class (except for one who confessed that she always turned off animal shows when they featured birds) moved to the window.

"Oh, *I* see it!" exclaimed the most enthusiastic, the one that liked *everything* in the course, including the quizzes. "*I* don't," mumbled the one with thick reading glasses, "I'll be lucky if I find the house."

After a few minutes of pointing out ("No, to the *right* of the tree . . . the *maple* tree . . . no, the *blue* house"), most of them claimed they saw my owl and drifted back to their seats.

It wasn't until I got about halfway through the hour and a half of class that I began to feel uneasy. Going on about Don Quixote's sincere, yet wrongheaded misperceptions, compared with the views of the other characters and of the reader, I asked with a rhetorical flourish, "Who's the crazy one anyway? Are the characters who see the windmills for what they are really superior to our hero? Is he any less brave just because it's not really a giant he's fighting?"

Some students raised their hands to offer an answer, but I was too busy with my bird to call on them. The owl was still there. It hadn't turned, hadn't moved a feather. It was also taking no notice of the pigeons resting comfortably beneath its talons. Even owls don't hang around quite this long, I thought, nor do threatened pigeons. With the heat of embarrassment building up, I tried to return to Don Quixote's dilemma.

Because of my hobby, I had acquired an entirely undeserved reputation on campus as a bird-watcher, enough that people described sightings of unusual birds at their feeders, sometimes flapping around the fax machine or trilling birdsongs to me as if I could give them an ID. I had never sought this distinction, but I could see now that whatever credibility I had was at risk.

"I still think he's a fool," said one student. "A windmill is a windmill."

"I don't," protested another. "After all, he thinks the windmill is a real giant, and he takes a big chance when he attacks it."

The class was over. Telling them to think about the problem for next class, I offered no final statements, no blockbuster bons mots.

Before they left, some of them took a final polite peek out the window.

"It's a *fake!*" said Jay's smirking office mate Vinnie, waiting in ambush as I stepped out of the classroom. "Yup," said Jay, "Ceramic, or wood, or something . . . been up there for at least seven years!"

"Seven years, huh?" I mumbled, fiddling with my dog-eared *Quixote*. "Really?"

"Oh, yes . . . it's supposed to fool the pigeons," chortled Vinnie, digging Jay in the ribs with his elbow.

"Well, he fooled at least one," I replied with fake jollity, retreating down the hall.

"Hear you saw it *move!*" called Vinnie from behind me, as I tried to disappear into the crush of students gathering outside the classroom door.

At our next meeting my *Don Quixote* students, more tolerant of lunacy than most, were consoling when I confessed my error. But what's a windmill or an owl among literary sophisticates?

"I was wondering how long it was just going to sit there like that," admitted the enthusiast. "It was still there at three when I left my biology class!"

At the final exam, one student wished me a summer of "happy owl watching."

I've also received in my department mailbox advertisements for high-powered binoculars and for wooden owls "guaranteed to fool unwanted visitors," and I got an order form with Peterson's *A Field Guide to Birds East of the Rockies* checked off for me.

The owl still sits on the antenna, a daily reminder for me to stick to *Don Quixote* and keep quiet where birds are concerned.

Gilbert White's Selborne

Homer's Troy, Cervantes's La Mancha, Wordsworth's Windermere, Yeats's Ben Bulben, the Brontës' moorlands, Thoreau's Walden—all are places in this world so intimately associated with the spirits of their writers that it's impossible to ignore them.

Even with Turkish sailors on leave frolicking on the bastions, I couldn't look over the walls of Troy without imagining Helen there as Homer drew her, and the Trojan elders admiring her glory: "Terrible is the likeness of her face to immortal goddesses." Listening to the loud moor wind thrashing a pub sign, I could almost hear Heathcliff's frantic "Cathy!" And at Walden, where I walk regularly, I never escape Thoreau's view of it: every bay, every rock, every tree seems to speak with his voice, and for me it is a pleasure. He has, after all, traveled more in Concord than I have.

Alone in the hexagonal, thatched bird blind at The Wakes, Gilbert White's house in Selborne, England, I had a similar encounter. Listening to the beech tree scraping on the roof, watching the doves, the magpies, and the swallows, I found myself thinking much more about Mr. White than about the birds I was hiding from. The enduring spirit of Selborne, he tugged at my memories of his book, calling me back to his own vivid eighteenth century. Like White himself, Selborne resides in that familiar half-bird/half-book world.

The common ancestor of all amateur bird-watchers, of all chroniclers of the local scene, White was a vicar who couldn't help looking up from his Bible to watch the birds passing by his study window, and he still compels me to look with him.

In the famous letters of his *Natural History and Antiquities of Selborne*, covering the years 1767–87, he gives detailed descriptions of nature's round in this tiny village. With affection, he reports on voles and tortoises, bats and bees, plants and flowers, and especially on the birds, perhaps ancestors of the ones then darting in front of me, right through the bright patch at the doorway of the blind. I was in Mr. White's yard, borrowing a hideout built as he would have wanted it. And these birds, busy about his garden, his sundial, remained unquestionably Mr. White's birds.

I also felt this sense of "his" as I climbed the Zigzag Path up the "Hanger," the beechwood hill rising three hundred feet behind his house. With his brother, White himself cut this switchback trail that rises so gradually to the top, where he placed a welcome bench and a wishing stone. Geoff, then a toddler, easily climbed this tame track, certainly less precipitous than other mountain trails we have hiked. Yet like the sacred way to Delphi or the sodden sheep run up Yeats's Ben Bulben, it was a special track, where White still outpaces his friends, his "junto of Zigzaggians." To climb this trail is to join his junto.

For the best part of his seventy-three years, White lived in Selborne, and a glance at a table of his life's events shows the irresistible tug of this particular location: 1720, White born at Selborne vicarage; about 1729, returned to Selborne; 1751, became curate in charge; 1763, became owner of the vicarage where he was already living and where he remained until his death in 1793. Serving as pastoral assistant at the church where his own grandfather had been vicar, White lived his days simply—visiting the sick, performing rituals of birth and death, tending to the poor, preaching, writing, and with greatest pleasure, observing the natural goings-on about him.

Although he attended Oxford and periodically stopped in on other places, he rarely went far astray. He was subject to coach sickness, and his horse would, by report, make Don Quixote's rickety Rocinante seem fit for the Preakness. White traveled a good deal in Selborne, and in the *Natural History* he tells a traveler's tale.

When I first began reading him, his book seemed dry, retaining too many vestiges of the "Garden Kalendar" it grew out of, too much unadorned recording of natural facts: rain tables for 1779–87, hatching dates for swallows, summer bedtime for swifts (8:45). I was missing the philosophical lifting off of a Wordsworth or a Thoreau. I looked for aphoristic insights, pithy lessons read in the book of nature, and found instead simple descriptions of what really happened: "Swans turn white the second year, and breed the third" or "Weasels prey on moles." He rarely preached, rarely used techniques for driving me to go on. But I had read about him so many times that I was determined to keep reading.

And gradually, as with the ascent up the Zigzag Path, I reached the bench at the end. I wasn't exhausted, I wasn't elated, but I was satisfied. Maybe it was the very lack of designs on me that gradually took hold. White is not dramatic; he is not a gusher. He rarely raises his voice. He is, however, an appealing companion: friendly, informative, and perfectly willing to let readers wander off the trail.

I had to slow down enough to look with him, to study his words as closely as he studied the world he was recording, but I was not at all forced. White is as much an attitude as a text. He teaches how to look. He teaches tone. He leaves his ego out of it.

Eventually his style, both prose and personal, makes its claim—his sure confidence, as when he argues that worms stir in every month of the year, "as anyone may see that will only be at the trouble of taking a candle to a grass-plot on any mild winter's night," but tempered by his self-deprecating honesty, as when he chides himself for assuming that ousels migrate southward: "Common ingenuousness obliges me to confess, not without some degree of shame, that I only reasoned from analogy." His gentleness is also appealing, as when he contradicts the observations of his correspondent: "But I cannot quite acquiesce with you in one circumstance . . . it is not the case with us."

He is above all calm, patient, willing to get up early, stay out late, sit for long stretches. His vigils are silent, private, as the natural world gradually reveals itself to him—in the field, up a tree, under the hay in the barn, beneath the eaves. As naturalist Richard Jefferies says in an essay on White, "For it is in this quietness that the invisible becomes visible."

But should the invisible choose to remain invisible, the infinitely curious vicar takes steps to search out its secrets—dissecting an owl or a viper, measuring the parts of a dead moose, examining the craw of a buzzard, tearing out roof tiles, digging up a mud bank where he thinks martins might be dozing in their "hybernacula."

He is also a fine writer, in a style uncluttered and unaffected. His words, his phrases, his images seem always right. He seeks the right vocabulary, the "granivorous tribe" of hard-billed birds; the "exasperated matrons" of the barnyard attacking a sparrow hawk; the sedge bird with the complex message, a "delicate polyglot." He also captures what he hears, making sounds themselves live— the fern owl like the "clattering of a castanet," or the "quick dactyls" and the "slow, heavy embarrassed spondees" of his own experiments with echoes.

Influenced by Latin, the Bible, and the rhythms of religious poetry, his words strike with force, as when he describes a titlark befuddled by a cuckoo: "The dupe of a dam appeared at a distance." Or when he observes maternal devotion among the birds: "This affection sublimes the passions, quickens the invention, and sharpens the sagacity of the brute creation." Like the writing of his contemporary Samuel Johnson, his words often demand and usually reward close attention.

Attempting to capture sights and sounds with only words, his comparisons are imaginative, original. His pet tortoise, Timothy, moves forward at a pace "little exceeding the hour hand of a clock," and he hides during rain:

> No part of its behavior ever struck me more than the extreme timidity it always expresses with regard to rain, for though it has a shell that would secure it against the wheel of a loaded cart, yet does it discover as much solicitude about rain as a lady dressed in all her best attire, shuffling away on the first sprinklings, and running its head up in a corner.

Then there are the insects that "sport in the sun-beams of a summer evening" or the rooks, looking like fast-moving planets, with "a flight of starlings for their satellites."

But these stylistic achievements probably would not have been appreciated by so many decades of readers, nor would his words have been so influential, were it not for the appeal of the way he lived. He was busy, but never so busy that he missed the life before his eyes (as I too often do). Reading his book is like taking a walk with him. "Look!" he says, "Over there!"—a "gossamer shower" of cobwebs "twinkling like stars." "Listen!"—a swallow taking a fly, "like the noise of the shutting of a watchcase."

He invites us to the satisfactions of living on a small scale, sharing in observations that may lead to nothing grander, but that "by degrees may pave the way to an universal correct natural history." Of Joseph Addison, C. S. Lewis said, "He is an admirable cure for the fidgets." Gilbert White could cure Addison's fidgets.

White has been criticized for narrowness of vision, especially for ignoring the grand events of his time—the Seven Years' War, the American Revolution—and for rarely referring to people. True, he does seem somewhat reclusive, but it's also true that in this *natural* history he did not intend a historical or social chronicle, nor do we have evidence that he was unfriendly or withdrawn. Hints elsewhere in his writing suggest otherwise. He was remarkable, though, for his concentration, for his focus on those small things he gives his time to, as a clerihew by Edmund Clerihew Bentley lightly suggests:

> "Dinner-time?" said Gilbert White,
> "Yes, yes—all right
> Just let me finish this note
> About the Lesser White-bellied Stoat."

White inspires those drawn to close-up views. James Russell Lowell said that reading White made him want to get up and go outdoors.

White is father to those who work in nature's laboratory, to those who seek to understand the crucial interdependencies of life, and especially to those who make the natural world the subject of their prose. He is also father to those writers who focus on a single place, sinking ever deeper into the native soil. His injunction that "every kingdom, every province, should have its own monographer" suggests that sometimes staying put is preferable to traveling and may be just as compelling a journey.

Darwin compared visiting White's house to visiting a shrine, but I had little sense of pilgrimage until I entered the churchyard and stood by the yew tree, already a thousand years old in White's time.

He wrote often of this tree, and there it still stands, with six props supporting its weary limbs. Mr. White's yew. From there I went to the rear of the twelfth-century church, to the gravestone that reads simply,

```
GW

26th June

1793
```

Then I heard a noise like the shutting of a watch-case. Mr. White's swallow? Was I just imagining the sound as he had written it? He would certainly expect me to check it out before I left.

With the Twitchers in England

Before I discovered English birds, I discovered English books, and it was there I began to appreciate the birds. In a translation of the Venerable Bede, I read about the little bird who flies in one door of a mead hall and out the other, his time within compared to our brief lives. In Anglo-Saxon I sailed with the exiled and lonely wanderer, cruelly tormented by the calls of curlews, gannets, and gulls, and then I followed skylarks, cuckoos, and hawks through the centuries to modern birds like Robert Bridges's nightingales that share with us a "dark, nocturnal secret."

I did get glimpses of the living birds of England, but I usually dashed by them to the library, to Chaucer's "smale foweles" who welcome his Canterbury pilgrims and to his many others: the birds who rescue the dreaming hero of *The Book of the Duchess* from despair by singing "mery crafty notes"; the gabby eagle in *The House of Fame* who lifts the terrified "Geffrey" into the heavens, all the while delivering an untimely and funny lecture on gravity; the feisty birds in *Parliament of Fowls* who stake their claims to the hard-to-get eagle. Chaucer liked birds, and I liked Chaucer.

It wasn't until a sabbatical year in England, while auditing a lecture on medieval manuscripts, that I found myself more interested in the real birds outside the window. I remember sitting in the basement classroom, taking notes on the Peterborough *Chronicle* as huge gold chestnut leaves tumbled and scraped across the parking lot. "I'd like to be out there," I thought. But from age five, through a Ph.D. and then into teaching, I was accustomed to suppressing such autumnal yearnings, so I focused again on the script spread before me. It was schooltime.

Then the thrush called out a trilling melody, a clear, unmistakable song worthy of Tennyson's "wild little poet," and again I looked to the chestnut trees. "You're on sabbatical," I said to myself. "You *can* be out there if you want to be. No one *expects* you in school this year. No one's taking attendance." I left that class not much enlightened on manuscripts but planning to spend some time looking at those "smale foweles" of England that I had been reading about for so many years.

Living beside a country canal, my desk facing a field open to the horizon, I didn't have far to look for the birds. Resident swans drifted on the gentle current, sometimes scrambling up the slope for a handout from Rosy, an octogenarian neighbor who had grown up on a narrow boat and knew her swans well. They hissed at me. In the spring, cygnets nestled on the mother's back, cupped between lifted wings. Wood pigeons settled in the fluttering elms across the canal, while the hunter's pickup truck idled quietly. Down the canal, moorhens nested in the thick reeds while collared doves and cuckoos called over the village.

In the evenings an owl of unknown identity—unknown to me—hooted, and almost daily an iridescent kingfisher darted right in front of me, down the middle of the canal and under the old stone bridge. Blue tits and English sparrows fluttered about our garden, eating my packaged basic floral mix before the seeds sprouted and dodging our neighbor Albert's wily cat.

Over the years after that sabbatical, I added more birds to my English life list: magpies and wagtails, jackdaws and rooks, grebes and gadwalls, a gray heron who strolled in front of us down the canal towpath. I found Shelley's skylark at Stonehenge, and from coast trails I spotted countless gulls, calling as they called to the lonely Anglo-Saxon wanderer. Even on the way to the library, I stopped to notice the birds. I also noticed that I wasn't the only one noticing.

It's hard to come up with a private sighting in England, where the birds are among the best-watched in the world. Bookshop shelves sag with old and new books for young and old, for amateur and professional birders, on every imaginable way to think about a bird. Individual species get whole studies (*The Finch Handbook*), as do habitats (*Birds of the Wetlands*) and family backgrounds (*Owls: Their Natural and Unnatural History*). Birds are studied for what you can do with them: raise them (*The Aviculturists' Handbook*), cage them (*Cage and Aviary Birds*), hunt with them (*Falconry and Hawking*), or simply watch them, producing an infinity of guides from pocket-sized to unliftable folios. In *Birdwatchers' Britain* you can place birds on detailed Ordnance Survey maps, with little silhouettes spotting them on particular trails and designated hills.

Throughout the country, aviaries and wildfowl havens nurture living birds, while museums and schools study stuffed ones. At the Natural History Museum in Oxford, crowded glass cases of domestic birds line the balcony, cases of foreign birds edge the ground-level railings, and special displays focus on avian ancestry and evolution. "*Archaeopteryx*'s ribs were non-ucinate with no sternal articulation," says the poster. Also at this museum is a small case containing the head and foot of a dodo, extinct through slaughter since the seventeenth century and an unhappy contrast to the swifts of the Museum Tower, lively residents who are the subject of a whole book, *Devil Birds: The Life of a Swift*.

You can also watch birds on the radio. The first time I came upon one of these expeditions, I thought my radio had tuned out, until I listened carefully and heard an occasional crack of a twig, a rush of wind, a bleat, then a moo. This was a regular program where an expert guides a companion through a favorite birdy site. Long silences, punctuated by natural noises, are interrupted by an excited "Look . . . over there on that fence post . . . a gray wagtail!" or "Now there's a very agitated tree pipit," followed by a short, whispered report on the status of the locals. Sometimes the guide uses birdcalls, but usually he knows the area so well that the expected birds turn up unsummoned for their radio broadcast. The companion—quizzical, attentive, respectful—is a surrogate for the at-home bird-watcher, tiptoeing around the kitchen not too far from the radio.

Watching birds and their ways has an illustrious genealogy in England, reaching back through such observers as Julian Huxley, Richard Jefferies, Charles Darwin, and Thomas Bewick to the eighteenth-century parson Gilbert White, direct ancestor of the radio guides.

Current enthusiasts stay informed about birds still on the wing through periodicals, national and local organizations, and an intricate living grapevine made up of bird clubs, newspapers, radio, and TV bulletins: "Another good shearwater year, with reports still coming of sightings in West Cornwall—twenty Cory's, two great, two Balearic, and three sooty" or "A subadult male red-footed falcon is on Mendip near Cheddar."

One summer, comedian and bird-watcher Bill Oddie conducted a commercial television tour of his favorite birding sites, a program to which the glossy TV guide gave a page and half, with text and close-up photographs of ten birds plus Oddie.

After this TV tour I read Bill Oddie and David Tomlinson's *The Big Bird Race*, an account of a bird-watching competition between two observation teams: Country Life versus the Flora and Fauna Preservation Society. "Superbly fit, their reflexes honed to a knife-edge of paranoia," writes Oddie, each team recorded as many birds as possible in twenty-four hours—a "Big Day" in bird talk. In mock military prose, the authors describe the experts on the team, the high-powered scopes, precision maps, Land Rovers, speedy cars, and walkie-talkies: "Dead Auk to Hawkeye, are you receiving me?" They tell of setting out in the dead of night, staffing reconnaissance and backup teams, and plotting an itinerary around bird-rich East Anglia. A 155-species Big Day by the Country Life team was enough not only for a victory but for an English record.

Reading about so many birds I had never seen, especially the nightingale I had waited two evenings for in a damp thicket (in honor of Keats), I decided to try for my own Big Afternoon in East Anglia, at Cley Next the Sea. Though I would certainly fall far short of the 155, I might at least get to hear the bird the poet describes with such affection:

In some melodious plot
Of beechen green, and shadows numberless,
Singest of summer in full-throated ease.

Then again, maybe I wouldn't.

With its sodden feet on the low-lying coast, Cley is one of the birdiest places I have ever been, for the concentration of both birds and watchers. It's a major lure for "twitchers"—watchers-on-the-run, with nerve-ends anticipating the chance of sighting a life-lister. At Cley, twitchers come close to outnumbering the twitchees, hiking boardwalks to hides where they rub crowded benches smooth and speak in coded mumbles. At gift shops they buy bird key rings, bird place mats, bird scarves, bird socks, and bird tea cozies. A café near the shore papers its walls with pages from the *Field Guide to the Birds of Great Britain and Europe*, and along the shingle sea-bank, watchers gather in alert clusters, all dressed in earth colors.

At the Hotel Harnser, named for a heron, a stuffed bird presides over the registration desk where, while signing for a room, you can buy local bird lists and bird postcards. The dining room is also avian, with portraits of birds and cases of stuffed local specimens keeping them in mind at breakfast, dinner, and supper. Table conversation? "Can you imagine that fool trying to flush that redshank?" or "Are you sure that was a *bird*? I think it was a rabbit." From our waitress I learned of the unexpected visitor from Siberia, the little whimbrel feeding near the Salt Shed. This little "superbird" or "crippler" had already made it into the London newspapers and was posted on the BBC. Twitchers lurched toward Cley.

Following directions to the Shed, we hoped not to miss the whimbrel, but there was no chance of that. Lining the road was an unmistakable flock of twitchers—standing, sitting on the shoulder, lying on the verge, kneeling on cars, all of them focusing binoculars, telescopes, astronomical starfinders, cameras, zoom lenses, on the tiny brown-streaked bird poking among the weeds with its long, curved bill. Quietly they took detailed notes, some in columned ledgers like accountants' records.

"Lovely little bird, that, isn't it?" said one, and offered me a look through his high-powered scope. I saw the bird eye to eye and once more felt the thrill of a "first," and in this case maybe an "only." Probably blown off course by a storm, this little bird is no more common on the American side of the Atlantic than in England. After one more long look, I listed him in my *Guide*. Like Ross's gull back home, he had come to me.

I didn't get to see Keats's nightingale—that is, I "dipped out," or missed a sighting—but I did wonder if anyone might appreciate an "Ode to a Little Whimbrel."

As I write this in our Oxfordshire apartment called, with good reason, "the Stable Flat," geese, ducks, and a flock of bantams peck noisily about the barnyard. A hen cackles over a recent egg, and every once in a while, with no clear cause, the bossy cock summons his harem and his chicks. Chucking and clucking, he ruffles them into a corner of the cow pen, letting them go only when they all submit to his strutting authority. Pity the hesitating hen. I think of Chaucer's Chauntecleer, who struts cockily up and down his barnyard, the embodiment of arrogance, looking like a "grim lion." Again I appreciate the poet's linking of the living and the literary world, his evocation of a real place, of real inhabitants, for his tales.

More than any other place except maybe Thoreau's Walden Pond, not far down the road from my Massachusetts home, England allows me to indulge both my vocation and my avocation. I haven't the time or the temperament to be a full-time twitcher, but I have tracked down many an English bird since that liberating thrush in the chestnut tree. On my next trip I'll return to Cornwall, where last time I stayed so close on King Arthur's literary trail that I missed the shearwaters at Tintagel.

Very Like a Bird

Sabbatical is a chance to quiet down, a time to explore side trails, so on my most recent one, spent at home, I signed up for a course in "drawing from nature," hoping to join a tradition reaching at least as far back as the hunting scenes in the Ice Age caves. I would learn to draw birds, and as a bonus I'd improve my chances of recognizing them later in the field. I'd learn to look less out of the corner of my eye and more directly.

The result of my first assignment—a chickadee that looked like a rabbit with feathers—almost drove me to giving free street-corner lectures on Shelley's "To a Skylark." One thing was certain. My artistic skills had not improved since elementary school, where my suns blurred green into my skies and my people stood stiff like coaxial balances, those scrolly designs spiraling in mirror patterns off a central pole (which I was always pretty good at drawing with a ruler).

I did discover, though, that I draw better upside down— with the subject being copied upside down, that is. I was amazed to see that faced with a picture postcard standing on its head, my left-brained, managerial notions of what a bird should look like got short-circuited and my right brain had its artsy-craftsy way with my pencil. My inverted chickadees emerged much less like rabbits than my upright ones did, and my eagles, sometimes looking lovable enough to pet when drawn right side up, developed an upside-down glare. "That's not a bad bird!" said my ever sympathetic instructor.

Out in the field doing my weekly assignments, however, neither the birds nor I stood on our heads, so my old left brain plugged in again and my chickadees started wiggling their noses. Bad birds. At an iced-in sanctuary, I found a busy feeder swaying from a maple limb and tried the required "gesture sketches" of birds—hasty squiggle marks intended to capture, according to my teacher, the "essence of birdness" in each bird. This was easy for her to say, since her most random squiggles looked ready to take off.

My gestures showed that I had a cold and that my fingers were aching as I tried to draw birdness on the slippery page. The haste in my squiggles suggested that what I wanted most was to go home, but I knew that such minor inconveniences would not deter a true student. I remembered reading of the fetid air, stinging midges, deer-flies, and vicious wood-ticks in the heronry Edward Howe Forbush once explored. I thought of George Miksch Sutton crawling through a narrow log, occupied by spiders and mice, on his way to a turkey vulture nest. He endured first a daddy-long-legs crawling across his nose, an irritant he crushed by pushing his face into the wood. Then the mice raced with sharp feet across his back and under his shirt. When he finally reached the mother vulture, she hissed, then vomited decayed flesh at him.

How could I let a mere wind chill deter me from my feeble efforts at the bird feeder? When I thought of Emma Turner, who proudly camouflaged herself so well under heaps of litter that the birds often took her for rubbish, or of Jonnie Fisk, a personal friend, who at age seventy-three spent five months alone in a sixteen-by-twenty-foot rock cabin so that she could net the birds flying through her canyon, I blew on my fingers and renewed my pursuit of a gesture-chickadee.

I forced the fluttering pages down and sympathized with the chaotic flurry of feathers struggling to the feeder. The birds were having a hard time, too. Inspired as I was by my predecessors, the essence of birdness continued to elude me for at least another half hour, and my dashed-out lines meant to represent wings in motion, tail feathers gliding, finally looked more messy than birdy. Gestures of the icy wind. The only real clue to the scene was the umbrella feeder, some of whose essence of feederness I did nail down on the page. The birds, meanwhile, moved in minuscule sequences of poses, like fast-forward fashion models, and blustered from feeder to bramble to feeder too wildly for me to catch. When they all got blown simultaneously into the bushes, I gestured my respect for Edward and George, Emma and Jonnie, and hurried to my car.

By the time I got home, my fingers were able to unclench the steering wheel and turn the stove knob for tea. Warming up, I checked out the feeder just outside the kitchen window, but, like the feeder at the sanctuary, it rocked and bounced frantically in the wind. It was birdless at that moment, but I knew that at least the house sparrows and the juncos would return when it settled down, and I had to get that assignment done. So, in the relative calm of the next afternoon, I delivered the baby to her nap, set up two kitchen chairs at a respectful distance from the window—one for me, one for my pad—then supplied myself with a field guide, binoculars (for those subtle details), and coffee.

I settled in, sharp pencil poised. I sipped my coffee. I shifted in my seat, repositioned my pad, did warm-up doodles. I sipped more coffee. I waited. No birds. All the time I was sitting there, not a single bird came. Maybe our neighbor had a better seed mix, maybe the birds peeked in and saw me sybaritically lounging there, but they never did show up. I was reduced to copying a junco from a postcard propped upside down against the instant coffee jar.

That night I took on another of my teacher's suggestions— "draw birds from a television program"—but the topic, the excessive killing off of wildfowl during migration, left me mostly with a page full of approximate ducks dropping out of the sky and many dead ones on the ground. Still lifes they were, but Chardin had no reason to be concerned.

My options were not up, however. Seeing the evidence for my plight at the feeders, both outside and at home, my instructor told me to try stuffed birds. After all, bird artists used to kill their subjects to keep them still for the portraits. Audubon wired them into picturesque poses. "Then you can take as much time as you need," she said.

"That's the secret!" I thought to myself as I headed for Harvard's Museum of Comparative Zoology. In the consoling emptiness of a weekday afternoon, I wandered up and down the aisles among the glass cases. As in some ghostly Eden, birds in various poses, of various sizes, in various stages of preservation stared at me glassy-eyed. I searched for a simple one. My pad wasn't big enough for the herons or the cranes, and the elaborate stripes, spots, streaks, and designs of the spring warblers were obviously beyond my talents. But with the naïveté of a novice, I finally settled on the smooth, simple patterning of the cedar waxwing, perched forever on the edge of her empty nest.

One hour later she was still perched, keeping her part of the bargain, but I was wondering why I had thought I might capture any of this bird's subtle elegance. She didn't have obvious spots or streaks, no assertive colors or intricate patches, just a silken gradation of soft tans and dusks from her perky top feathers to the yellow tip of her tail. With my lead pencil all I could capture was her dark face mask, not her face. I couldn't get her tail to hang over the nest at the proper angle either, and the beak, perfectly still, refused to look like hers—she developed a most un-waxwing-like smirk. Even her feet escaped me until I hid them among the tangles of her nest.

Birds are not easy to draw, I wisely concluded, as I left the museum with neither weather nor television nor subjects to blame. I shouldn't have put myself through this feathery ordeal to make this discovery. I had already read what I didn't need a sabbatical to discover: like any other art, drawing birds takes time—hours, days, years, lifetimes of observation, reflection, practice.

It takes knowledge of anatomy, of how a bird's sternum relates to its clavicle. It takes knowing a primary from a secondary, a scapular from a covert. It takes volumes of rejected sketches, forests of pencils. More than a sabbatical.

Although I flinched at Audubon's methods ("The fact is I was anxious to kill some twenty-five Brown Pelicans"), I came to appreciate his energetic images, with the birds always *doing* something. With greater respect, I traced the meticulous lines of Louis Agassiz Fuertes, an amateur field naturalist who painted birds so accurately that he was relied on by the scientists of his day and who also illustrated editions of Burroughs, Burgess, and Forbush.

And I admired still more Roger Tory Peterson's ability both to capture the "essence of birdness" and, at the same time, to select

the markers necessary for people like me to know what we're looking at. I appreciated the sentiments of artists like Terence Shortt,
who found sustenance in the plenitude of birds, "grateful that
there are more than can be comprehended in one lifetime."

And I saw that it takes a special kind of patience, a special
kind of love, to draw birds well, as Frank Chapman said of his
friend Fuertes:

> *His concentration annihilates his surroundings. Color, pattern, form,*
> *contour, minute detail of structure, all are observed and assimilated so*
> *completely that they become part of himself and they can be repro-*
> *duced at any future time with amazing accuracy.*

These talents and sentiments were so far beyond my range
that I almost gave up; but just at the right moment I gained some
courage from the youthful admission of Dr. Alexander Wilson,
one of the greatest of the early bird artists: "I declare the face of an
owl, and the back of a lark, have put me to a nonplus."

His problems suggested that maybe I should give up on the
birds for a while and take an artistic step backward to a basic drawing course, where I would try to develop an artist's eye, a view of
the world made up of line, shape, shading, perspective. I'd try at
least to *see* Fuertes' colors, patterns, forms, and contours. Before I
took on another waxwing, I'd learn to coax at least one stubbornly
flat, blank page into 3-D. Fruits, wine bottles, and models wouldn't
take flight, and I could at least learn to capture the oval in a hen's
anatomy.

After much erasing, my bottles gradually turned out better
than my birds, and my people looked less like coaxial balances.
But with every new subject to be drawn, every miscast shadow,

every misplaced nose, I appreciated even more the artistry of the cave dwellers and their descendants. With an even more admiring eye, I saw their birds come to life before me—singing, courting, feeding, attacking—on surfaces often far less cooperative than my pad.

One spring day near the end of my sabbatical, I tried to draw a flock of red-breasted mergansers swimming in a partly frozen harbor. With perfect symmetry they moved forward, then made sharp about-faces, apparently pursuing a school of tricky fish. By a sympathetic observer, my gesture sketches might be taken as birds, not driftwood, and at least one merganser, with his tousled head feathers, looked slightly "rakish," as Peterson describes him. But the best of all my merganser sketches turned out to be the placid seascape that remained when the birds dived, all at once, out of sight.

Sabbaticals may be a time for exploration, but they can also be a time for discovering limitations and thus appreciating more fully the achievements of others. Peterson's merganser is the really rakish one.

Meanings Within

Reading John o' Words Again

S tanding on the porch at Slabsides, John Burroughs's woodsy
New York retreat, I peer through the iron grating into the
dimness. Gradually the chairs, window seats, counters, cabi-
nets, yellow birch pillars, and curious wooden shapes become
visible. I squint to find his desk, the one with tripod legs of bent
sumac.

Having seen so many pictures of him, particularly in his
white-bearded, prophetic period—Burroughs perched on his
"boyhood rock" in Roxbury, New York, Burroughs reading roman-
tically by candlelight, Burroughs examining a blossom with a magnifying glass, Burroughs scanning the hills for a bird while shading
his eyes with a wide-brimmed hat—I can almost see him sitting
there. Alone at his rustic desk, he stops his pen or looks up from
his pad only if a nuthatch raps at his door or a robin scuttles into
her nest under the eaves.

Sitting on the porch steps, I can imagine myself one of the
many visitors posing with the patriarch. My hair is lifted in a 1907
do, my dress long and flouncy. Maybe I'm a "Wake-Robin," a Vassar student and member of the bird club named after his first book.

Burroughs was one of the most popular, most widely read writers of the fifty years between his first nature book and his death in 1921 at age eighty-four, and he remains a presence in the long sequence of natural history writers. But at this time he is enduring an eclipse. When I received a collection of Burroughs essays as a gift, I gave him more attention than before, and I enjoyed what I discovered. First of all, his selection of subjects is wide and varied—philosophy, literature, travel, aesthetics, animals, geology, insects, and farming among them—but the birds are his favorites, and it was these that brought me to his door at Slabsides. I had come to shake the hand of "John o' Birds."

And I had come to meet the writer. As much as I was pleased by his birds, I was more fascinated by his apparent ease at making essays of them. It was this writer's art more than anything else that led me to visit his birthplace, discover his houses, peek in his windows, size up his desk, sit at his grave. As he himself said, "One does not truly live his experiences until he transmits them through the point of a pen." I was curious about what happens when John o' Birds becomes John o' Words, about the way he pens his transformations into prose.

First of all, he writes about real birds, not imaginary birds, plastic birds, human birds, or sentimental greeting card birds. "I paint the bird for its own sake, and for the pleasures it affords me," he said. The birds fly and fight, sing, mate, nest, and die in his pages. He goes into the fields an "interested spectator of *life*." In a typical encounter, a little red owl feigns sleep until Burroughs pulls him rudely from his nest: "Then, like a detected pickpocket, he was suddenly transformed into another creature," the feisty owl and the nosy writer face-to-face.

A nesting chickadee, already known to Burroughs, rests quietly until a curious Vassar girl comes too close. "Why, it spit at
me!" she says—a "little trick" that Burroughs had expected. He
then doggedly follows a drake returning to his abandoned mate
through the vineyard, across the fields, down the highways, over
the railroad tracks, and up the lane, and he describes the bird's
determination, "as if an invisible cord was attached to him."

But not all his encounters are so charming. A particular
junco, daily companion at a study where Burroughs often wrote,
disappears unexpectedly from her nest, and he discovers her
"stone cold" eggs the following morning and grieves for her. He
also watches with both interest and sympathy as a black snake
slowly devours a catbird.

He writes exactly what he sees and prides himself on going
to the fields without a notebook, with no planned use for what
he sees: "Studied the birds? No, I have played with them, sum-
mered and wintered with them, and my knowledge of them has fil-
tered into my mind almost unconsciously." Burroughs approves of
amateurs.

But he does not approve of falsifiers, however affectionate—
of those who turn the hummingbird's eggs blue, make starlings
into songsters, place English cuckoos, larks, and wood pigeons in
the North American woods, set the partridge drumming out of
season, cause the bluebird to chant hymns, or metamorphose the
web-footed cormorant into a bird of prey. For Burroughs, poetic
license does not allow for lies.

And more sharply, in his 1903 article "Real and Sham Natural History" he challenges the writers he calls "nature fakers,"
those who force the natural world to do their artificial bidding—

birds conducting kindergarten classes, holding clan meetings, committing operatic suicide. Burroughs thinks such caricatures do the natural world a disservice and insists that nature "unadulterated, unsweetened" is far more interesting without reduction: "In fact, nature study is only science out of school."

Always reflective, always an "interested spectator," even "of the workings of his own mind," Burroughs had the scientist's eye and the poet's heart: "The problem of the essay-naturalist always is to make the subject interesting and yet keep strictly within the bounds of truth." The writer must take hints from nature, itself working "in the direction of concealment," must dig through with the pen to whatever is there—the beautiful, the horrible, but most important, the true: "The facts are not falsified; they are transmuted."

Sitting at his desk, he discovers meanings in the birds outdoors, finding "more in the telling than in the thinking and the feeling." He finds "unbounded delight" in the morning song of a veery and inspiration in the arrival of a bald eagle: "What attracted him there, attracted me." He finds a picturesque analogue for his own creativity in his study, where "while I am busy with my books and my writing, the birds are busy with their nest-building or brood-rearing."

Soon after his mother's death, the song of a fox sparrow provides consolation: "How it went to my sad heart." In the last year of his life, suffering the loss of friends, family, and his own health, he still responds to the song of the hermit thrush: "I had almost forgotten how divine a strain it is." Sometimes he is drawn to longer thoughts, thoughts of birds as "fellow passengers" who share with us the revolution of the planet: "We are making the voyage together, and there is sympathy between us that quickly leads to knowledge."

But perhaps the pleasure Burroughs derives most frequently from seeing his birds and then writing about them is in reliving his experiences. In this sense, he who writes lives twice. Ever nostalgic in the true sense of "aching to return," Burroughs also looks to the distant past, and on that route too the birds trace a flyway for his imagination and lead him to the writing. He helped me understand some of my own urge not only to look, but to write down what I saw. He shows how the birds and the writing work together.

In his early book *Wake-Robin*, he explains that writing "enabled me to live over again the days I had passed with the birds and in the scenes of my youth." As a youth he had, for example, simply noticed a small bluish bird, but it took the adult writer to know what to make of the black-throated blue warbler he could now name: "It was a revelation. It was the first intimation I had had that the woods we knew so well held birds that we know not at all."

Burroughs's birds, then, are not scientists' birds, not moralists' birds, not the birds of the insensitive surveyor who goes to the field and sees only the field. His birds become birds of literature, transformed by his pen.

Ironically, he apologizes for his lack of skill as a writer:

> But I really have no dexterity as a writer. I can only walk along a straight, smooth path. Of the many nice and difficult things I see done in prose by dozens of writers I am utterly incapable. What I see and feel I can express, but it all must be plain sailing.

This may indeed be a reasonable assessment of his own "limited range" compared with the vast landscapes of Homer or Shakespeare or the depths of Thoreau, but it also might be a salvo of *sprezzatura*, self-deprecating nonchalance, from one who elsewhere comments on how much study and discipline he puts into his writing. Plain sailing is hard work, and he knows it.

Just how clumsy is Burroughs as a writer? A thoughtful reader who wrote often of his own literary genealogy through Montaigne, Johnson, Emerson, Whitman, and even the dangerously powerful Thoreau ("Reading him is like eating onions"), Burroughs knew the challenges of nonfiction. He explains that without "poetic forms" to mask empty-headedness, the prose writer "has no such factitious aids; here he must stand upon his own merits; he has not the cloak of Milton, or Tennyson, or Spenser, to hide in."

So, unmasked, uncloaked, Burroughs writes with beguiling simplicity, not cluttered by jargon or encumbered by pretensions. He uses the right words in the right places and says what's on his mind. Hoping to discourage a flock of English sparrows from devouring the buds on his plum tree, he throws stones at them, concluding with a flurry of assonance, "And a hint is as good as a kick with this bird." Or with an alliterative punch, supported by preacherly doublets, he laments the extinction of the passenger pigeon: "Death and destruction, in the shape of the greed and cupidity of man, were on their trail." I can almost hear him pounding the pulpit.

Plain though his style may be, though, his similes strike fresh. The chickadees are "like the evergreens among the trees and plants. Winter has no terrors for them." After hearing a collector brag about his cache of bald eagle eggs, he remarks with Thoreauvian

irony: "I felt ashamed for him. He had only proved himself a superior human weasel." Or with biblical enthusiasm: "The house wren
is the one bird whose cup of life is always overflowing."

He describes the natural world through the familiar sights
and sounds, the literary and religious sensibilities of his readers;
his repetitions make connections and move the writing on, as in
his use of the word "tell" in a passage on nature:

> *I have loved Nature no more than thousands upon thousands of
> others have, but my aim has been not to tell that love to my reader,
> but to tell it to the trees and the birds and to let them tell him.*

His monosyllabic, almost hammering, conclusion here
drives his point home. But his confiding afterthought, "I think we
all like this indirect way the best," typically softens it.

He transforms the natural world into essays, his words
bringing the birds to life. But as he knows so well, they do more
than this: "People admire my birds, but it is not the birds they see,
it is me."

Like all familiar essayists, Burroughs is finally his own main
character, the true central point of interest, though he seems to be
writing about anything but himself. The drake makes his dogged
way back to his mate, but the equally dogged, somewhat foolish
and ever curious John Burroughs pursuing him on his long and
devious route is the one who keeps us reading.

The writer translating into prose the joy of the veery's song
is the one capable of joy. The observer appreciating the "primal
sanities of Nature" is one of the sanest among natural historians,
who without trying tells more about himself than about any of his
subjects. It's more the Birds o' John than John o' Birds. As he

acknowledges, "Nature has nothing to say. It all comes from within."

Sitting alone on Burroughs's boyhood rock just above his birthplace in Roxbury, the same spot he so often used as a vantage point, I think of his relative absence from the present literary landscape and try to explain it to myself. I know that literary prominence runs in phases, that rising stars and eclipsing reputations are part of the literary universe, that the literary essay itself, at times so belletristic, lost some of its preeminence over this anxious and war-torn century. I know also that younger writers often engage in a ritual "parent killing" to clear themselves some writing room. But I think it's time for a new look at John Burroughs.

No postmodernist, no stranger in a strange land, no cynic, no designer of self-consuming artifacts, Burroughs writes with a clarity of style and a concern for his readers that might well be a valuable antidote for some of the prose written now, particularly in the schools. Maybe his focus on chickadees and thrushes makes him seem not quite smart enough for our media-blasted pseudo-wisdom; maybe he's too warmhearted, coming across as sentimental in a time that mocks such feelings. Maybe he doesn't stand up well enough to the politics of John Muir or the profundities of Thoreau.

But I do have some hope for him and for us, when I think of my mostly teenage English literature students who always surprise me when they pick, say, Alexander Pope or Samuel Johnson as their favorite, or who actually *like* contemplating the lessons against greed and stupidity in the medieval *Everyman*, or who don't know yet that it's unsophisticated to fall in love with Malory's Lancelot, "the courteoust Knight that ever bore shield"—mere words on the printed page, alas.

Burroughs, the person and the writer, has much to say. He cares deeply for things worth thinking about, things more threatened now than they were in his more lavish natural world, and he expresses this caring well.

I look out across his grave to the old, worn Catskills reaching gently to the horizon. I am disappointed that there are no birds but the ones I'm conjuring up from his essays. Then a chipmunk scrambles onto the flat stone wall at the foot of the grave. When it spots me on the rock it freezes, but finally it sits back on its haunches, seeming also to look toward the hills. No, I don't think a congenial Mr. Chipmunk is sharing a literary moment with me, certainly not at this particular location. But I abandon my thoughts about literary fame and fortune and I watch, glad he's there.

I remember Burroughs's account of a wary chipmunk nestling in his pocket, and I remember this quotation:

> *The most precious things in life are near at hand, without money and without price. Each of you has the whole wealth of the universe at your very door. All that I ever had, or still have, may be yours by stretching forth your hand and taking it.*

His call to simplicity and to enjoying what life offers right before our eyes seems more than ever a call worth hearing. I would also like to stretch forth my hand and borrow his pen.

La Colombina, Non È Andata Bene!

I had read about the Scoppio del Carro—the Explosion of the Cart—long before Easter, so I knew it was one of Florence's most popular annual events. I was aware of its deep roots, reaching back to the medieval Holy Saturday custom of delivering sacred light from house to house, and I knew that it had come to commemorate the Resurrection. So when a glossy brochure announced in English, "In any case, all our joyous feelings and expectations will culminate at twelve noon that day during mass at the Duomo," I had to include it in our long list of things that couldn't be missed during that sabbatical year in Italy. An academic year in Florence is a year studying history.

So Geoff, Julia, and I got up at sunrise, put on woolens, boots, and slickers, and walked the two chilly, showery miles to the piazza at the Duomo, Florence's main cathedral. By nine o'clock we joined the already large crowd pressed close to the rain-soaked barricades. The mood was festive; even the carabinieri patrolling the open space in front of the Duomo were smiling through the rain. I bought Julia a pink Easter bunny balloon, also smiling. Geoff amused himself by climbing the barrier rails. The explosion would be at noon.

Having done my research, I knew what to expect. Timed with the "Gloria in Excelsis" of the mass at the main altar of the Duomo, the archbishop's flame would ignite a small model dove, powered by a rocket, that would then take a swift course high on the cable stretched down the nave, out the door, and into the piazza. Before doing a sharp about-face back to the altar, the dove, the *colombina*, would spark a sequence of fireworks laced in tiers around the thirty-foot-high carriage, or *carro*, right there in front of us.

I had seen pictures of this rolling tower being delivered in pomp to the Duomo by two pairs of white oxen. With promises of the spinning and sparkling of the Catherine wheel, the crackling of the rockets, and the blossoming of the pennants and banners from the top of the tower, I had lured the kids on our long, wet walk. We and all the others in the rapidly growing crowd were ready for the big show.

At ten o'clock things began to stir. To our right I got a glimpse of brightly dressed drummers, acrobatic flag throwers, white oxen with flowers laced to their horns, and finally the wide-bodied carro, ambling into the piazza. Excited, I told Geoff and Julia to get ready. Geoff climbed the rails, and I stood Julia on the top bar. This is when the carabinieri began moving sections of the barricade, including ours, to make way for the entourage. The earliest of us got pushed off and then aside, protesting all the while, and when the barrier was pulled back into place, the latecomers made a sudden rush to the front, forcing their way into better positions.

Feeling my hands being pulled from theirs, the kids screamed from within the crush, but when a boy with an American accent called out, "Bambini! Bambini!" an oasis opened up gently around them. They calmed down. As Julia's balloon drifted over the baptistery, I could see that we were now a good six rows back from the action, and no one was about to give up such hard-earned advantage.

Already upset that my husband and I had apparently mixed up our meeting place, and angry at the bullying crowd, I prepared to leave. I could see very little; the kids could see nothing.

"Do you want to get on my shoulders?" a tall girl in a University of Toronto sweatshirt asked Geoff. Not really wanting to leave, Geoff quickly agreed and got lifted to his perch above the crowd. "My name is Jeanne," she said. "What's yours?" Geoff introduced himself to the top of her head. Not really *wanting* to leave either, I hoisted Julia onto my own shoulders and resigned myself to the hour and a half of uncomfortable waiting yet to come.

To pass the time, I listened to my ever-closer neighbors, mostly English-speaking students, including Jeanne, a Canadian music student, as they chatted about schools in Italy, anatomy textbooks, Brunelleschi's double domes, and—when subjects wore thin—the weather in England. Hearing me explain to the kids about the carro, they began to quiz me. "What does it mean?" asked the English microbiology student. "What's going to happen?" asked the American boy who had earlier rescued the bambini. And from a girl who drifted in and out of the conversation, a laughing, "*Why* am I here?"

As efficiently as possible, with Julia asleep resting her chin on my head and Geoff craning for a better look at the oxen, I told them the carro's long history. I told about the carro itself, a recollection of the wagon once used for Holy Saturday processions in Jerusalem. And I told them about the symbols—the Florentine lilies, the Pazzi dolphins, the fire, or fireworks, of the Resurrection; the gray, then red smoke, possibly suggesting the triumph of love over the deathly ashes of Lent. You can take the teacher out of the classroom . . .

For those who remained curious, I told about the oxen, ancient symbols of patience and tireless strength, and I recounted how one year the city tried to save money on renting them. Officials thought the $10,000 fee was too much and advertised for substitutes. They received only one call, reportedly from a farmer who disappeared when asked to verify that his oxen were not just white cows. Apparently the white oxen we would be seeing were the only ones left in Tuscany.

The students looked interested. I realized that I liked having an audience; I had been away from teaching for almost a year. Besides, I was reminding myself of the things that made this spectacle more than just a tourists' fireworks display.

Urged to go on, and eager to comply, I told them about the dove, added during the reign of the Medici pope Leo X. An ancient symbol of purity and peace, reminiscent of Noah's reconnaissance bird, the dove carries an olive branch and brings a message for the local countryside, telling of springtime and resurrection but also foretelling the harvest. If the dove flies well—if it makes it to the carro, ignites the flashy display, and returns to the altar, fruitful crops of grain, grapes, and olives are more likely. I knew that "La colombina, è andata bene?" ("has the dove flown well?") remains a serious question for many in Florence and vicinity and that a bad flight presages disaster. But I don't think I realized how serious the question remains for some; I was simply relaying information I had gathered at the library.

I gladly quieted down when the drums rolled and we all tried to catch a glimpse of the multicolored flags tossed high in the air. Geoff gave us some play-by-play. Just after 11 o'clock, a man in a cherry picker eased the Catherine wheel onto its perch on the carro, and the onlookers, now crammed into every possible cranny, pushed forward against the unyielding barriers. I felt Julia's weight lighten on my shoulders as a short man behind me got pressed off balance against my back. He righted himself too soon for me. Julia woke up and screamed for her lost balloon.

Shortly before noon, a clash of voices to our right made us think the colombina was on the wing early, but the noise was simply a loud protest aimed at a young woman who had decided to view the finale from her boyfriend's shoulders, thus blocking the view. Like a reluctant swimmer, she slipped down into the chilly sea of disapproval.

As the seconds ticked to noon, my back aching, I stared at a short span of cable stretched from the darkness of the church to the carro until it became a blur, as if someone had strummed it. The tall ones tried to focus cameras over the heads of those in front of them. With hope, I took several one-handed shots of heads and ears. Occasionally a flag lifted into view. We all leaned forward and slightly to the left, all off balance, no one capable of taking a step, let alone falling. Checking my watch, I imagined the archbishop lighting the flame at the altar.

The bells of Giotto's campanile rang out the Resurrection, and the fireworks began to spark and bang—sharply, one by one, in sequence around and around the carro. The happy crowd applauded. The kids clapped too. A tiny flame snaked purposefully up from tier to tier, setting off each row in turn, and finally sparking the wheel into a whirling, smoking, exploding victory. The church facade echoed each degree of crescendo, and red smoke drifting high from the almost invisible carro obscured the geometric patterns of pink, green, and white marble. The stone clerics in the lowest niches, hands raised in blessing, seemed to wave the smoke away.

After the four loud reports of the final rockets, after the rows of white waterfall sparklers began to flicker out, Geoff looked down and asked, "Where's the bird, Mom? I didn't see the bird!" I didn't see the bird either, but given my vantage point I wasn't really expecting to. Then the others began to ask, "Did you see the dove?" "Where was the bird?" "Dov'è la colombina?" Jeanne asked an Italian woman pressed next to her.

And then I heard a man shout out the line that, up to then, I had only seen in books: "La colombina, non è andata bene! . . . non è andata bene!" "The dove has not flown well!" I couldn't see the person shouting, but he sounded distressed. This was not the way they had planned it, I thought, as I pried Julia from my shoulders, lifted Geoffrey down from Jeanne's, said my thank-yous and good-byes, and made my way back through the dispersing throng. It had been a big show out there on the rainy piazza, but not the one they had planned.

On the way home I heard again that the dove had not flown well. And then I learned that the dove had not flown at all. Inside the Duomo she was indeed set in motion by the archbishop's flame, but she flew only a moment, then stopped. After just a few feet her rocket exploded, and the dove hung by her claws above the disappointed sighs and murmurs of the congregation.

In spite of all efforts to prevent a failure, including retro-rockets on the dove and remote-controlled fireworks on the carro, the bird had not completed its mission. This flop seemed to me a simple misfortune, one more piece of evidence, even an amusing one, that the best-laid plans go oft awry.

The next day I read in the newspaper the reactions of the Florentines, and many, I confess, surprised me in the depth and sincerity of their despair Some pointed darkly to two of the colombina's memorable failures—in 1939, at the start of World War II, and in 1966, the year of the destructive Arno flood. But to me the scale of these foreshadowings seemed out of proportion. World War II and the most devastating flood ever to hit Florence? And the colombina's flight had something to do with them? What could possibly come in the following year?

"The colombina has betrayed Florence!" one grieving spectator told a reporter. "It's a massacre . . . a sign of thoughtless and unholy times!" declared an all too deadly serious observer. And from a more hopeful moralist, "It's a sign that Florentines should work hard to do better . . . manna from heaven will not help them." I could see that my tourist attraction, my check-off in a list of things to do that year, was to many others more than a show at the piazza.

Outside the church, the Scoppio del Carro was more a social experience than a sacred one, like the chaotic playfulness of Florence's annual mud-splattered Renaissance soccer game. But inside, for many the bird represented true prayer, a sincere supplication for God's blessing on the city.

The previous year the dove had successfully flown *to* the carro but had been unable to return, an omen that many saw darkly fulfilled in the ensuing twelve months of parking problems, lack of runway space at the airport, soccer losses, unsightly restorations at the Piazza Signoria, toxic air, evictions, drug use, and general immorality in the city. This year, with no flight at all to lift their hopes, some frightened onlookers predicted even worse consequences for the next twelve months.

I found myself sympathizing with those for whom this bird carried so much symbolic weight. I saw that my Easter extravaganza was their hope for God's grace—grace denied this year. But in spite of this I felt more in agreement with one Florentine realist quoted at the scene: "It's a sign that the rockets weren't very good."

It seemed to me that these believers were asking too much of this little mechanism, feathered or not. With so much significance to bear—so much past and present, so many Florentines, so many country folk, so many wet, cramped, and moody tourists, it seemed almost predictable that this little bird would cover only a few feet of cable before she sputtered out, exhausted. She would need more than rockets to carry so heavy a burden.

Given our efforts to get there and to stay there, my day would have been more complete if we had witnessed the full round-trip flight of the dove, but for many of us in the piazza the fireworks, the rockets, the whirling of the Catherine wheel, the flowering of the pennants and the banners were both a relief and a celebration—no matter how remote the control switch, no matter how disabled the bird. Even without the bird, we got our share of the tradition, the picturesque, sparkling part, and we left the dripping piazza satisfied. For others the colombina delivered a dark message. Our show-and-tell tourism had crossed flight paths with a living tradition.

Venice: A City on the Wing

The last time I was in Venice, I must have ignored the pigeons. I wasn't really interested in birds, least of all in pigeons, and besides, I had already seen lots of them—pigeons in Paris, pigeons in Rome, pigeons in Trafalgar Square, pigeons in my front yard devouring my high-powered Rebel grass seed. I had a color photograph of myself in London with pigeons walking on my head. As far as pigeons were concerned, I would probably have agreed with James Thurber: "Nobody and no animal and no other bird can play a scene so far down as a pigeon can."

But since that first trip to Venice, I had taken up bird-watching, and I had read Jan Morris's *Venetian Bestiary*, where she claims that Venetian pigeons are special—pigeons worth a second look: "The pigeon is, if not actually sacred, at least highly respected in Venice." I was curious about what might stir so much respect for a pigeon.

As our water taxi burbled into the dock at San Marco, I began to wonder what degree of semiconsciousness could have allowed me to ignore the pigeons my first time in Venice. They were everywhere—thousands of them—gray, dull, everyday pigeons.

At our feet they reluctantly yielded a path as we walked into the grand piazza. At one moment the facade of the cathedral would be on display in all its ornate glory; at another it would be totally blanked out by pigeons. On balconies, pediments, cornices, and the bell tower they lodged, looking like rain-stained finials. Any sharp noise sent them into a flurry of flight. The pigeons aloft swept down to the piazza; the ones on the piazza lifted and banked into niches, shaping themselves back into stone.

Thirsty pigeons clustered around fountains and, always hungry, stalked the tourists on the piazza, a pigeon per square foot. It was impossible to take a step without almost stepping on one. As if by agreement, they monitored the pigeon-food vendors strategically placed around the piazza, then pursued the little plastic corn bags in tumbling headlong masses, shaking down the purchasers for the last kernel.

Tourists posed with pigeons following a corn trail up one arm, over their heads, and down the other arm—pigeon aureoles. They knelt in pools of pigeons where one scrambling bird couldn't be distinguished from another, the kneelers themselves finally lost among the feathers.

Sometimes the birds relinquished their territory, as when a determined man with a purpose other than pigeons strode diagonally across the piazza without a moment's hesitation, regularly slapping a rolled-up *La Stampa* against his thigh. Among the pigeons he seemed to have a reputation—they gave him a rare right-of-way.

Toddlers too sent the pigeons into hasty motion, but outmaneuvering toddlers is obviously part of initiation into Venetian pigeonhood. Assaulted by a little girl's screaming rush, they moved aside just enough to let her pass—a crew of bullfighters toying with the bull. When Julia let her corn bag trickle, the birds reversed the pack and did the pursuing themselves until, hip deep in pigeons, she squealed and dumped out the whole bag.

As I looked down from beside the bronze horses high on San Marco's loggia, pigeons moved in kaleidoscopic patterns as they broke up and regrouped across the piazza. Like tiny tesserae, mosaics in motion, they clustered at the feet of feeders and then dispersed. Seen from that height, they seemed to mimic the motion of the tour groups, themselves clustering, then moving out in ragged unison. Pigeons trailed the feed bags. Tourists chased guides carrying multicolored umbrellas, batons, and something even a pigeon wouldn't follow, a smiley-faced orange impaled on a stick and wearing a gondolier's straw hat.

Venetian pigeons go to bed at night. You can walk across the piazza after dark and not see a solitary one. Our hotel keeper explained that at sundown they retreat to roosts throughout the city, and at sunrise they take flight back to their day of tourists, toddlers, and corn. Our hotel room looked out on a busy pigeon commuter route where, every morning, they flapped noisily down the narrow passage just outside our window. Back to work.

Seen through the slightly open venetian blinds, they looked like the shadowy flashing images of silent films or the bird flight in children's cartoon flip books, flicked into broken motion.

According to Jan Morris, pigeons might be taken seriously in Venice because Doge Enrico Dandolo chose a carrier pigeon to deliver news of his victory in Constantinople, or perhaps because of the old tradition of releasing doves over the piazza on Palm Sunday. For centuries Venetian pigeons have carried both secular and sacred messages.

But in spite of such a long tradition of respect, not everyone in Venice is a pigeon fan. Disturbed by the damage done to equally venerable Venetian buildings, some critics argue for pigeon control and are charged with going so far as to lace seed with poison.

These pigeons may well need help from the insurance company they have been known to advertise—Assicurazione Generali—their advertising work often pictured in Venetian photo reproductions. In the early morning the company quickly poured out seed in the shape of its initials, and for the moment that the seed and the feeding pigeons stayed in place, the letters formed a huge AG in piazza writing. In a trattoria, I also saw a blown-up photograph of a more ambitious "Coca-Cola" pigeon script— critically unacclaimed contributions to Venetian piazza art.

I *did* see other birds in Venice: magpies, sparrows, and four swans in the outer reaches of the lagoon near the seaside tourist enclave of Iesolo, high-rise and glossy. I also heard a dove there, sounding sad, perhaps lamenting the heavy settlement of this once-desolate and bird-crowded fishermen's outpost. And throughout the city itself were caged parakeets squawking through the bars, canaries trilling from the upper balconies, and gulls perpetually coasting over the Grand Canal or perching on striped posts at the gondola docks.

I was almost too aware of birds in Venice. One rainy day I watched a sparse procession of tourists shuffling by like carnival monks in their just-bought pink, blue, green, and polka-dot plastic raincoats with pointed hoods. Some even crossed their arms and tucked their hands up their sleeves. Seeming lost in dreary meditation, they didn't notice they were being watched by the many birds so near to them. That day most of the tourists were inside, waiting out the heavy rain, and seed was in short supply, so the pigeons looked down from covered perches or from trees just above the procession. The gulls watched too, comfortable on rain-slicked pilings, one for every bird. Suspended animation.

I also took note of the flocks of man-made birds in Venice—on rooftops, facades, ceilings, floors, and pedestals. And I took into account feathers in general, adding to my bird lists the winged lions of Saint Mark, portrayed throughout the city. Venice seemed a place on the wing.

Six-winged angels rose over pediments; winged evangelists hovered atop towers. I discovered the wings on the Torre dell'Orlogio, a clock tower in the piazza, and in a vestibule dome of San Marco I sought out the birds in the Creation mosaic—the dove brooding upon the water, avian creation hovering above the fish in the sea. I was happy to notice that even the soul God granted to Adam is portrayed as a tiny man with prominent wings. In the Noah mosaics, birds enter the ark two by two, and Noah releases a dove over the floodwaters.

Farther inside the cathedral, I looked down rather than up and found in the twelfth-century mosaic floors depictions of cocks, herons, vultures, peacocks, and winged reptiles.

Jan Morris suggests that the Venetians themselves have a special fascination with birds, possibly because of the legendary founding of the city in A.D. 421 when the bishop of Altinum was guided by a flight of seabirds to settle in the unlikely lagoon. And she suggests that the Venetians see themselves as similar to the birds—all being lagoon dwellers precariously settled on the land, constantly threatened by the sea. I had no such historic explanation for my own fascination; I just couldn't stop looking for them.

As I thought more about the birds myself, I wondered too if the obvious delight with wings and the devotion to the pigeons may be at least partly accounted for by Venice's unsteady turf. The high waters, or the *acque alte*, and the flood of the Adriatic, make constant claims to the lagoon and to the land Venice rests on so unsteadily. It is a city with spongy foundations, as its wavy floors, curving facades, and tipsy towers attest. Venice lives threatened with sinking. The original campanile, a symbol of Venetian stability, toppled in 1902, and the entrance to San Marco has now subsided well below piazza level. I wondered if the city yearned for wings to rise above the flood and so, like Noah's dove, escape a watery demise.

As I began to seek out other explanations, I decided it might be time to leave. But even on our last night in Venice, enjoying the easy stepping and the coo-less quiet, I found myself thinking idly of the birds that weren't there.

"What's that, Mom?" Julia asked as she ran to a far corner, toward a stone fountain. I followed her and discovered two barefoot little Venetian girls busily putting wind-up plastic doves into flight.

The Tune in the Tree

C*hick-a-dee-dee-dee!* said the juniper tree, a sharp command slicing through the crackling air. Experienced with chickadees by then, I knew immediately what bird it was, but looking into the setting sun, my eyes watering in the January wind, my fingertips numb, and my binoculars frozen on fixed focus, I had a hard time finding it.

I was already blasé enough about chickadees not to spend much time looking for them, but there, at the end of a peninsula stretching into the Atlantic, where the bay was blown smooth, snow spiraled and swiveled into wild drifts, and the shoreline shattered into a puzzle of jagged ice, this bird's call was reassuring. It was a sign of life in the desolation. Except for one herring gull pumping without effect into the gusts, this chickadee was the *only* sign of life.

When the juniper called again I found the bird, hanging upside down on the rattling bush like a forgotten Christmas ornament. He rocked gently in the breeze as his call pierced the air.

I was happy to see and hear the little bird that stays in Massachusetts on days like this—the justly chosen state bird—but

I must admit he wasn't as eloquent as Ralph Waldo Emerson's chickadee on a similar January day, a true fellow traveler that did all but invite the writer to supper. Emerson's bird sings,

> *As if it said, "Good day, good sir!*
> *Fine afternoon, old passenger!*
> *Happy to meet you in these places*
> *Where January brings new faces!"*

Had my bird been so talkative, I might have looked among precocious parrots for identification, but my chickadee's simple *chick-a-dee-dee-dee* left me with no doubts.

I wish other birdsongs were as easy to match up with their birds. I can pick up the deep melody of a robin or the raspy jeer of a blue jay, and on a spring day I immediately recognize the clarion call of the cardinal that nests on my hill; but when I get much beyond those, birdsongs give me trouble.

Having been on field trips with experts who hear a slight squawk in the distance and immediately name the squawker, and who often know well beforehand what bird is likely to be in the next tree, I've witnessed how valuable birdsong is to identification in the field.

"Sh-h-h! Hear that?" asked the leader of the owl prowl through the dark and snowy woods.

"Hear what?" I wondered.

"A barred owl," he announced, "at about a hundred yards and moving in."

At that moment I heard nothing but the soughing of the breeze through the pine needles and the squeaking of snow beneath heavy boots. I finally did hear the owl in a nearby fir tree, but if the bird hadn't called long enough for my guide to tune me in to the "barking" sound with a pronounced *-aw* at the end, I would have missed it entirely.

Wanting to improve my ear, I bought the set of Cornell Laboratory bird recordings and dutifully played them through, but I made it only twice all the way from "p. 1, Common Loon" to "p. 180, Chestnut-collared Longspur" before I gave up. Unlike a colleague of mine, who listens to bird tapes every day while driving to and from school, I got lost in the jumble of page numbers, bird names, and sample songs and traded my tape for "golden oldies" somewhere around "p. 82, Laughing Gull." Waiting in line at the copy machine, my colleague can trill a convincing yellow warbler and call up a tremulous screech owl. More than some others in the line, I admire his achievements.

But as much trouble as I have with recordings, I have even more with visual representations of songs—the field ornithologists' line sketches, fanciful doodles, and sophisticated audiospectrograms. In the sonograms of the introduction to *Birds of North America* I can hear the "automobile horn," the "ticking clock," and the "wolf whistle," but the skid marks recorded by the Brewer's sparrow do not sing to me at all.

Sometimes verbal descriptions help, especially if I've already heard the bird, and I can try to distinguish a buzz, a slur, a gabble, a rattle, or a lisp. I may even recognize a flutelike sound, a reedy note, or the rasp of a door hinge, and I think I could also pick out the song of the Henslow's sparrow, Peterson's choice for "one of the poorest vocal efforts of any bird . . . a hiccoughing *tsi-lick*." But how does a "gossipy" song go, or a "silly little outburst of ecstasy"?

Longer imitative phrases and lines can get me closer to the right singer—the "please, please, pleased to meetcha" of the chestnut-sided warbler, the "old Sam Peabody, Peabody, Peabody" of the white-throated sparrow (at least in New England), the "teacher, teacher, teacher" of the ovenbird, or the unmistakable announcement of the chickadee.

But neither is this system totally reliable, given the difficulty of translating songs into words. For example, in English the chiff-chaff sings, rightly, *chiff, chaff,* but in German it says *zilp, zalp,* in French, *tsyip, tsyep,* in Spanish, *sib, sab,* and in Icelandic, *tsjiff, tsjaff.* To be understood, the bird has to sing in the right language to the right listeners.

Further illustrating the translation problem, Edward Howe Forbush discusses the American bittern's love song as the loud "sucking of an old wooden pump" and offers a long list of descriptions: "punc-a-pog, ugh-plum-pud'n, glump-te-glough, gung-gi-um, dunk-a-doo, kunk-a-whulnk, umph-ta-googh, slug-toot, quank-chunk-a-lunk-chunk, punk-la-grook, and waller-ker toot," all supposedly variations of "I love you" in bittern. It seems to me that a bird seduced by a "quank-chunk-a-lunk-chunk" might find "slug-toot" a bit abrupt, but then I'm not the bittern being courted.

When I turned again to the professional students of song, I studied diagrams of the "tracheobronchial syrinx" that produces most birdsongs, and I found a definition of song as primarily the patterned "vocal display" of the male bird, usually during breeding season. I learned some additional purposes for song—warning intruders about territorial limits, establishing pecking order at the food supply, claiming command, maintaining family or group bonds, expressing satisfaction. And I discovered *types* of songs—whisper songs, subsongs, antiphonals, duets, night songs, flight songs.

These serious listeners also study the songs of adopted birds, deafened birds, birds in solitary confinement. And they calculate yearly and daily song cycles, reporting on discoveries like the brown thrasher's uttering 4,654 song units in 113 minutes or the male red-eyed vireo's belting out 22,197 songs in a single day. One musical analysis of birdsong identifies "accelerando" in the wood warbler's song, "crescendo" in that of the Heuglin's robin-chat, and "diminuendo" in the song of the South African misto seed finch.

After this effort to learn about birdsong, I became much more alert for a warbled "no trespassing," or "I'm available," or "I'm hungry" in the woods. But so far I still have trouble figuring out which bird is announcing what to whom. I do enjoy trying to name the singers and their tunes, but I'm inclined to agree with Robert C. Miller, who says, "Well, whether birds sing because they are happy, or hungry, or real-estate minded—sing they do."

My own ear guides me to the company of less scientific listeners who, like Emerson, discover artistic sentiments expressed in birds' songs. My ear may not be good enough to hear the avian subtleties of patience, faith, generosity, or love in the chirps and trills and *quank-chunk-a-lunk-chunks*, but I *think* I can hear springtime in the cuckoo's song, as Beethoven did in his Pastoral Symphony, and I can certainly enjoy the lively mockingbird on my neighbor's roof or in a good fiddle rendition of "Listen to the Mockingbird." And in the poets, I hear even better the meanings of the birds' songs.

The rhythms of Tennyson's European song thrush, for example, imitate what he hears as the repetitive, rhythmic, summertime joy of the real bird:

"Summer is coming, summer is coming
I know it, I know it, I know it.
Light again, leaf again, life again, love again,"
Yes, my wild little poet.

Walt Whitman's hermit thrush expresses strains of grief at the time of Lincoln's assassination:

Sing on, sing on you gray-brown bird,
Sing from the swamps, the recesses, pour your chant from the bushes,
Limitless out of the dusk, out of the cedars and pines.
Sing on, dearest brother, warble your reedy song,
Loud human song, with voice of uttermost woe.

Not elated, not as imitative as Tennyson's "wild little poet," Whitman's bird sings a "reedy" song of sadness. Meaning is often in the ear of the poet.

On December 31, 1899, Thomas Hardy too turns to a thrush, this time to express his own despair, but to his surprise he finds relief in the song of the aged bird:

So little cause for carolings
  Of such ecstatic sound
Was written on terrestrial things
  Afar or nigh around.
That I could think there trembled through
  His happy good-night air
Some blessed hope, whereof he knew
  And I was unaware.

The bird's "ecstatic sound" offers unexpected hope, evoking happiness where Hardy had previously heard only misery.

Since I enjoyed making these connections between real birds' songs and the messages the poets hear in them, I decided to pass the idea on to my students by bringing birdsong tapes into the classroom. When teaching Tennyson's poem, I played a song thrush for them; when I taught Shelley's "To a Skylark," I played an accompanying lark.

When trying to capture the Middle English poetic debate between the serious, responsible owl and the joyous, frivolous nightingale, I created, with some difficulty, an antiphonal tape of the two birds. The poetry worked as usual, with the owl claiming that his voice is like a great horn while the nightingale's is feeble, like a single pipe—"Ho is ilich one grete horne, / And thin is ilich one pipe"—and the nightingale claiming superiority in song, bringing bliss to everyone, "Ac ich alle blisse mid me bringe. / Ech wight is glad for mine thinge."

But when I turned on the tape, with the owl hooting and the nightingale trilling a response, then the owl hooting, and then . . ., the undergraduates squirmed in their seats and the graduate students nodded, mostly in sympathy. Some things just don't translate, I admitted, and moved back to the birds on the page.

Those bird tapes were a short-lived effort to bring the real world into academe, filed away with my plans to mount a wall-sized collage picturing all the major writers in English and my annual required field trips to Walden ("I don't have a car" or "I work every night and on weekends, and any other time you might be thinking of" or "I hate Thoreau"). I finally retired the tapes, but I wasn't at all deterred from listening to what the poets might hear in the singing of the birds.

I may have no sympathy for dressing elegant black bears in tutus or tying "buckeroo monkeys" onto sheepdogs' backs in a mock roundup of errant sheep, but even without tapes I do feel the human emotion expressed in the dreadful carrion calls of the scavenger birds on the Homeric battlefield, in the sad crying of the gulls to the exiled Anglo-Saxon wanderer, in the vital melodies of multitudinous nightingales, skylarks, cuckoos, robins, crows, and yes, chickadees. The tiny bird in Seamus Heaney's "Song" sings, he says, "very close / To the music of what happens," and so do a lot of other literary birds.

In fact, focusing on the songs of these birds in literature has on occasion worked in reverse, enriching my experience of the real songs outside. I remember sleepwalking through a cemetery bird walk on a chilly spring morning when a full chorus of warblers in a cherry tree suddenly sang in delicate cacophony and, for the first time that year, I felt the arrival of spring, coming to life among the headstones.

And at that moment I couldn't help thinking about the famous birds in the opening lines of Chaucer's *Canterbury Tales* that "maken melodye" in their anticipation of spring lovemaking. Sounding like air squeezed melodiously out of a party of balloons, my cherry tree warblers joined happily with my memory of the poet's "smale foweles" in a duet I think Chaucer would have enjoyed.

Perhaps the most literary of my real singing birds was a trilling, rising, trilling skylark at Stonehenge. I sat on a toppled slab reading dutifully about Aubrey holes and hele-stones, tumuli and barrows, but my attention was more on the noisy little bird lifting into the slaty clouds. Knowing I was hearing what is— except for the nightingale's—the most *significant* birdsong in English poetry, I recalled the "Hail to thee, blithe Spirit!" of

Shelley's "To a Skylark," and I also remembered his supplication at the end of this often-taught poem:

> *Teach me half the gladness*
> *That thy brain must know,*
> *Such harmonious madness*
> *From my lips would flow,*
> *The world should listen then—as I am listening now.*

To me too the bird's song was an inspiration, but it was even more an expression of "gladness" because of Shelley's poem.

Naturalist John Burroughs complained that the poem is "needlessly long, though no longer than the lark's song itself, but the lark can't help it, and Shelley can." I think Burroughs missed the point. Shelley is carried to poetic ecstasy by the song and tries to capture the melody by imitating the excess.

Drawing on a catalog of verbal resources, the poet gets enticed into a competition. He greets the bird directly, he limns elaborate descriptions, he asks rhetorical questions, he reaches for sensual similes: "Like a high-born maiden," "Like a glow-worm golden," "Like a rose embowered," like a "Sound of vernal showers / On the twinkling grass," yet he fails to capture the bird's joy. Shelley finally acknowledges the superiority of the bird's song over his own poem. In song, the bird is his superior:

> *Better than all measures*
> *Of delightful sound—*
> *Better than all treasures*
> *That in books are found—*
> *Thy skill to poet were, thou Scorner of the ground.*

Even with Shelley's 105 lines, the skylark wins.

After my own experience at Stonehenge, also teased into gladness by the bird's persistent trilling, "To a Skylark" has never again been for me simply an "Eng. Lit. II" survey entry. Shelley, the bird, and I have that song in common now.

As for birdsong in general, I'll continue to study the audiospectrograms, to listen for the differences between mating and territorial melodies, to separate the purposeful slug-toots from the silly little outbursts of ecstasy. But I'll also simply try to listen better to the songs, paying close attention to what *I* might hear in them. As Emily Dickinson says about an oriole's tune:

> *So whether it be Rune,*
> *Or whether it be none*
> *Is of within.*
>
> *The "Tune is in the Tree—"*
> *The Skeptic—showeth me—*
> *"No, Sir! In thee!"*

The birds have plenty to say to one another, plenty that's worth listening in on, and if we listen attentively and with imagination they may also say something to us. Something worth repeating.

Life-Listing in Kenya

Long before I got there, I was reading about Africa. I was already inspired by Hemingway's love of its green hills:

> Now, being in Africa, I was hungry for more of it, the changes of the seasons, the rains with no need to travel, the discomforts that you paid to make it real, the names of the trees, of the small animals, and all the birds, to know the language and have time to be in it and to move slowly.

Passages like this, with their aura of adventure, their hints of heroism, made me hungry for Africa too, as did Isak Dinesen's exotic descriptions of Kenya:

> I had time after time watched the progression across the plain of the giraffe, in their queer, inimitable, vegetative gracefulness, as if it were not a herd of animals but a family of rare, long-stemmed, speckled gigantic flowers slowly advancing.

Giraffes? Vegetative gracefulness! Speckled gigantic flowers! I wanted to see all this. And I discovered even more to see when I finally got to Kenya and continued my reading there. In fact, lugging a small library, I read myself through my three weeks there. At dusty highway rest stops, in dimly lit old hotels, and by flashlight in the tent, I ventured even further with Hemingway and Dinesen, and then with Elspeth Huxley and Alberto Moravia. I probed with the tale-tellers, with Conrad, van der Post, Naipaul, and Updike. I heard the insiders' voices from the locals—Grace Ogot and Ngugi wa Thiong'o. And in the bush I explored with our guidebooks—*The Travelers' Guide to East Africa* and John G. Williams's *A Field Guide to the National Parks of East Africa.*

I read about lion hunts, coups, floods, peculiar diseases, dives on the coral reefs, herds of photogenic game animals, thorn trees, thunderstorms, migrations, restaurants in Nairobi, shopping centers, and siafu ants—not friendly picnic ants out for a peanut butter sandwich, but the military ones that march in long columns and devour any living prey in their path, including people.

But well read as I was, I still wasn't ready for the birds except as subjects of hunting yarns, the game fowl so eagerly stalked and shot by so many people in so many ways. Even the field guide to the parks devoted only about one-third of its pages to watching birds. Already needing a bookmobile to carry our personal library, however, we decided to give up our search for a bigger bird guide and set out immediately on a practice safari.

In Nairobi we outfitted ourselves for camping—a four-wheel-drive Suzuki with a specially designed collapsible tent mounted on the roof, nonperishable foods, jars of insect repellent, and for me a khaki safari hat with a red lion roaring on the front.

With these supplies, two pairs of binoculars, and our books, we headed to Nairobi National Park, only four miles from the center of the city, yet the wildest suburb I've ever been in. It took us about an hour to see just *how* unready we were for Kenya's birds.

Using our general field guide, we easily enough checked off kongoni, Thomson's gazelle, olive baboon, silver-backed jackal, and Masai giraffe. I was even able to claim for my life list an ostrich, racing us down a narrow trail right beside our jeep. But it was all the other birds—obscured in trees, rustling in dry grass, drifting overhead, singing unseen, or preening in full view—that eluded us and our books. I understood even better Hemingway's hunger to name *all* the birds, and I could see what drove Dinesen to such apocalyptic visions, but I couldn't get beyond what one editor called the "Oh my!" stage of bird-watching . . . or what I might better call the "Oh my! What was *that?*" stage. In my safari hat I may have been an upstart Teddy Roosevelt, but without a good bird guide I was certainly no Roger Tory Peterson.

When I couldn't come up with a name for the big gangly gray bird with red face mask, hawklike bill, black-and-white striped rump, and fancy feathers raining down the back of its head, I knew we were in trouble. Since it was about ten yards from us and illuminated by the late afternoon sun, no field mark on this bird was indistinct. In fact, standing over three feet tall, it stayed still long enough for a detailed drawing, even by me.

But riffling over and over through the pages, I couldn't find it in our guide. How could they ignore something so big? It wasn't until I slapped the book shut in frustration that I noticed on the cover the large-print reference to "Rarer Birds." The birds in this general guide to the parks were "rare bird" supplements to Williams's complete *Birds of East and Central Africa*. So we were prepared to check off the white-collared olive-backed waxbill, an "extremely local and uncommon bird in the forests of western Uganda," but not to name the plentiful secretary bird of Kenya, which this patient poser turned out to be.

Humbled, we returned to Nairobi and to the National Museum, where at the display cases I listed, described, and crudely sketched the more common birds of Kenya. And later that night I strolled among the aviary cages in the Norfolk Hotel gardens, sharpening my eye for the living birds hopping about in the ornamental greenery. In a Nairobi bookshop the next day we also came up with a colorful *Shell Guide to East African Birds*, and at last, with Williams's complete bird guide—with only one hitch. It was in German. Except for the alternative scientific and English names, the entire *Die Vögel Ost- und Zentralafrikas*, including the field marks, was in German. But, we decided, better *Die Vögel* and a dictionary than the white-collared olive-backed waxbills of Uganda.

On the Uhuru Highway, heading to the Rift Valley and Masai Mara, I flipped through the new book and wondered how far we could fly with our neglected college German. But now as I reread the cramped pages of notes that I kept for this early part of our three-week stay in Kenya, I can see yet another problem not apparent to me at the time. It wasn't just the birds and the German giving me trouble in Africa, it was Africa itself—unfamiliar, disconcerting, sometimes frightening in its vastness.

Rejecting group safaris, we traveled alone, and I was glad we did. But a safari hat, even with a roaring lion logo, does not a heroine make. I wasn't any Teddy R., upstart or otherwise. As Alberto Moravia says in *Which Tribe Do You Belong To?*, "African pleasantness has always something disquieting about it," and after hours and hours of driving down lonely dirt roadways, the flat horizon stretching 360 degrees around us, I understood better what he meant.

I paid close attention to the huge landscape, the unobstructed views, the isolation, and did my best to appreciate all of it. But having just flown from the infamous Northeast Corridor of the United States, one of the most occupied, obstructed, crowded places on earth, I also found it impossible to relax out there in the wide-open spaces. I remember a horrible thought that crossed my mind. Maybe I was missing the golden arches, the traffic jams, the company. I *couldn't* be yearning for a mall, could I? Maybe for too many years I had taught Conrad's ominous *Heart of Darkness*, the story of unspeakable violence wrought in the African wilderness, of evil deep in the human heart. Maybe I just had to give myself more time.

But whatever the cause, my notes reflect a peculiar and persistent abstraction from the immediate scene. I didn't write at all about those fears. Instead, sounding like some enfeebled specter of Thoreau, I repeatedly and without conviction waxed pseudophilosophical about the spiritual *value* of the wilderness. So easily spooked by the hysterical laugh of a hyena in the bush, so easily saddened by the devouring of a felled zebra, I wrote glibly of the "necessity for the primitive." I'm not quite sure whose necessity it was; probably not the zebra's. But I didn't seem to feel any need to make sense.

Watching the tall and graceful Masai, dressed in red, carrying only spears as they strode over the open, dangerous land, I remember worrying that they might be eaten by lions. But in my notes I wrote instead at least two Kenyan shillings' worth of clichés about "colonial versus tribal identity." What I was talking about, I have no idea. Would the lions have been less dangerous on tribal ground? Were the spears less lethal in a colony?

I know I was wondering about a lot of things there on that lonely, rutted jeep track, but I omitted most of the details that stirred such wondering. The notes rarely contain a vividly drawn picture. Birds' names flutter in and out of the crowded pages, but the birds themselves are vague, their colorful presences absorbed by the larger messages I seemed compelled to deliver—even to myself.

Strangely though, as I think back to that visit, picking up hints in my guide books, my slides, and even my notes, those birds are still there for me—still among the most indelible of my impressions in that most compelling land. Apparently I wasn't missing them completely. I just wasn't keeping a good written record.

I remember now, for example, on an island in Lake Naivasha, the moving tuft of tall grass that turned out to be the crest of a crowned crane. As I moved closer to the shore, easily ten more of these red, white, blue, and yellow waders stood half hidden in the reeds, unflustered by me or my camera. I loved seeing them, loved photographing them, but at the same time I was worried that the boatman who left us on the island would forget to come back. Part of me was tracking crowned cranes, another part was looking for shelter for a terrifying night. The boatman did come, but late enough into the dusk for me to convince myself that I was about to die there among the cranes. I did mention both the cranes and that missing boatman in my notes—part of the inventory.

I can also recall the peace of early morning coffee on the back porch of Keekorok Lodge in Masai Mara, while watching the multicolored sunbirds pressing curved bills into the crimson bougainvillea blossoms framing the roof. I now remember that particular Kenyan coffee as one of the most satisfying treats of that vacation, and I can still see the dancing of the tiny birds and the gentle fluttering of the red petals as they moved from blossom to blossom. *Nektarvögel*, said our guidebook. "Saw *Nektarvögel* at Keekorok," say my notes.

This same stinginess shows up in my Lake Nakuru notes, even though the place itself was the most generous with bird sightings of any place I have ever been. Here too are mostly names, some scribbled in German, awaiting translation. Lake Nakuru, described by Roger Tory Peterson as "the most fabulous bird spectacle in the world" and by Sir Peter Scott as "the finest bird lake I have ever seen," forced us to use all the guidebook pictures, all the descriptions of shapes, colors, and songs that we could carry. To identify every bird we saw, we could have used another bookmobile, preferably with a tape deck for recordings of their songs.

I have never seen so many birds so fast. Unless I intentionally focused on my sneakers or shut my eyes, it was impossible *not* to see a bird.

The famous flamingos were the least of my problems; hundreds of them were hard to miss. As we eased the jeep through the tall grass to the lumpy, sodden edge of the lake at Hippopotamus Point, the pink crayon streak in the field of my binoculars gradually emerged as a flattened raft of flamingos, and finally as single birds—many balanced stiffly on one leg, others busily prodding the milky water with heavy, downcurved bills. Wind gusts ruffled wings and tail feathers, causing a temporary teetering, and then a random two hundred, I would guess, lifted off and settled down again.

My notes do mention that lifting off, but it occurs to me now, as I recall that moment, that they looked like a pink down comforter shaken high into the air and slowly settling back into place. Too busy distinguishing the *gross* from the *mittelgross* flamingos, I couldn't take time out for a simile.

When we started looking more closely at the hundreds of other birds right in front of our jeep on the shore—a cacophonous congregation of field marks, too close for binoculars—our talents as listers got their biggest challenge ever. Birds dug long beaks into the mud, combed through the reedy grass, slapped at the water among the roots of angular trees, and tripped gently with long claws across flat, floating leaves. As at a tiny airstrip, some coasted in and hustled others into departing; many remained UFBs as we rushed, and failed, to name them. The colorful "Alkaline Lake" illustration in our English *Shell Guide* helped, but the canvas before us was more crowded, not so clearly laid out, not at all still.

With one of us calling out field marks and the other managing the book, our efficiency improved, but our German wasn't equal to the action. No sooner would I track down the field marks for the *afrikanischer Löffler* slapping at the water than several ibises— a *brauner Sichler* or an *afrikanischer Nimmersatt* or a *heiliger Ibis*—would wander out of the grass or from behind a tree. It took a while to be sure they were "glossy," "wood," and "sacred."

The sketches helped, and so did the descriptions, once we got them translated. When we distinguished the *kräftiger Schnabel* of one stork from the *riesiger Schnabel* and the *gelber Schnabel* of the two others, we were able to name the solemn birds standing stiffly in the water, like abandoned dock pilings: marabou storks, common at Nakuru and known to prey on weak flamingos.

I remember calming down, as I sat there on the hood of the jeep, trying to name *Vogel* after *Vogel*. Many of them got away without a name, but I still added more to my life list that morning

than at any single time before or since—among them, all those
ibises and cranes, plus squacco heron, white-necked cormorant,
yellow bishop, Egyptian goose, ground hornbill, pied kingfisher,
and long-toed lapwing.

Back on the road around Nakuru, the shimmering iridescence of a hoopoe crossed directly in front of us, almost touching
the hood of the jeep, and farther down, in the middle of the road,
strolled four birds side by side—big birds—unwilling to hurry, but
too hidden in silhouette for me to get beyond *gross* as a field mark.
Not wanting to frighten them, we stayed at a distance, and finally
we pulled off at another lookout point on the lake. I can still see
that party of four, looking like retirees out for an afternoon's constitutional, disappearing into the dusty haze.

At Nakuru, I was determined to name as many birds as possible, as fast as possible. And the lake was equal to any challenge I
might offer. I raced from bird to binoculars to books to dictionary
to bird again. I was in a big hurry, and I can even remember wondering *why*. Sitting on top of Baboon Escarpment, feeding cookies
to the friendly rock hyraxes and overlooking the whole expanse of
the lake, I wondered why I was life-listing as if *my* life depended
on it. Never particularly devoted to this ticking-off style of birdwatching, I know I asked myself why I was so obsessed with naming every individual in this land of bird plenty. But if I came up
with an answer at that time, it appears nowhere in my notes. Now,
thinking back, I think I can explain.

I can see now that naming the birds was a way of making the
persistent and nerve-racking strangeness at least partly familiar. In
the old routine of spotting birds, checking them out, handling a
guidebook with field marks and names, I was doing my best to feel
at home, to take Africa under my own wing. Maybe I also shared

Adam's imperial urge to name, and thereby to gain some control over, a world that so often seemed beyond my comprehension.

I can see now, too, that the birds usually helped to calm me down, helped to tame some of the wildness for me. Over time, they gradually eased my transition into real appreciation for what was passing before my eyes. The elephant, making slow progress toward the wall and toward me, seemed more congenial with one cattle egret riding on her back and another tripping between her feet. I was able to walk slowly back to the jeep. The malachite kingfisher . . . "Definitely a malachite?" "Right!" . . . brightened up the muddy hippopotamus pool where the huge graynesses looked at us and sank deliberately, exposing only half-moons of eyes and jittery ears.

Later, as I drove across a dry streambed on a dusty bush trail, a dark-eyed Cape buffalo glared stiffly, then lowered its head, snorted, and pawed the ground, threatening to charge. I remember the futility of rolling up my window and then the panic of lurching out of the rut, hoping the jeep wouldn't stall. I also recall, with some gratefulness, the yellow-billed oxpecker on the buffalo's cheek. That bird distracted me for a moment from my terror and allowed me to remember how to shift the gears.

At Nakuru, not long before our departure, I sat on a fallen log and scanned the lake while behind me a pink-backed pelican roosted calmly on a high branch. All of a sudden I heard a rushing through the leaves, and before I had time to look, a chattering monkey plunged from an overhanging limb and snatched for my camera on the log beside me. The monkey just missed the dangling strap, and as I grabbed the camera I noticed the pelican looking down from her branch, still calm. She looks amused, I thought, and so I took her picture. The monkey was too fast for a picture, but what I saw as the pelican's quiet benevolence kept me from being as frightened as I certainly could have been. I was probably also getting more accustomed to Kenya and its ways.

Perhaps fortunately, I never did become foolhardy in my new courage, as I saw some others do—the intrepid photographer in sandals advancing for a close-up of hyenas tearing into a fallen wildebeest, the bold adventurer scaling a huge termite mound for a better photo angle on a nearby herd of elephants grazing with their young.

But partly because of the birds, I did become more and more able to satisfy the hunger that had lured me to Africa in the first place. From the security of the jeep, my mobile safety zone, my querencia on wheels, I got better at calming my jitters and enjoying what I saw.

Only once did the birds actually *add* to my uneasiness—at Masai Mara—and that was mostly by association. One whole night, lionesses prowled noisily around our campsite. Sitting wide awake in the tiny tent perched on the roof of the jeep, we listened to their roars, like ominous announcements from a large vault. Our most lethal weapon was a bread knife. The lionesses came so near we could hear their throaty panting, and through the long night I actually came to distinguish individuals by the pattern of their roars and their breathing. Until they dispersed at dawn, I imagined them scaling the small ladder to our tent or simply leaping through the flimsy canvas.

We survived, having been in no real danger according to our jolly park ranger, who spent *his* night listening to Jimi Hendrix tapes in a wood-frame cabin at the campsite. Our night had been a surreal lion-Hendrix duet. "They don't eat people now," he laughed. "They have so many wildebeest!"

I was not so easily consoled, especially on the early game run the next morning, as I watched the vultures weigh down the tree limbs, coast fast and low across the bush, or stumble bloody beaked over mutilated zebras, gazelles, and wildebeest. Without much in my experience to compare them with, they seemed more than normally vulturous.

As I photographed them from the jeep window, I shuddered when I thought about the lioness with a private menu, an exotic taste for people. Where might she have dragged *us*? Would those birds be tearing at us now? But distinguishing the white-backed vultures from the lappet-faced did give me something to think about—other than dark imaginings about my own demise.

Even as I write this, I can see that those Kenyan birds remain vivid in my memory, if not in my notes. They fly back in huge numbers, part of an older, Edenic world of plenty in which I had a brief chance to share. Like Hemingway, I loved seeing them alive and at home, getting to know their names.

But I can now also see that, unlike Hemingway, I was unnerved by the torn storm clouds devouring the flat horizon and our empty road, by the stark warnings about elephants' food raids on incautious campers, and especially by hungry lionesses prowling through my night. So I was also grateful for the relatively simple, instant, and direct pleasure in watching the birds, giving some of them names, and enrolling them on my list. They gradually drew me from my rambling and vague philosophico-politico-envirospeculation, and from my disquiet . . . and they enriched my memories.

Now I see them. Tall, tiny, crowned, bald . . . flashing yellow, calling in a cacophony of voices, treading leaves, shimmering, brooding, soaring alone and in masses, enhancing already robust blossoms . . . *Wunderbar!*

Waiting for an Eagle

After bird-watching for several years, Frank and I had listed many of the local birds, plus other sightings uncommon for us, like the sacred ibis in Egypt or the Ross's gull at a nearby harbor, and I had begun to write about them; but strange as it was, we had yet to see a bald eagle outside a zoo. This was becoming embarrassing, rather like teaching Shakespeare without knowing *King Lear*. I knew the eagle was not your everyday bird, but we seemed to be claiming too much indulgence as "amateurs."

"If you feel like driving that far, you'll be almost sure to see one at Cobscook Bay in Maine," said a bird-watching friend. So in the middle of the spring semester we took a fast weekend off from preparing for classes and correcting compositions and sped up the coast to a public park where the eagles are known to nest.

Skidding in tennis shoes through the winter-tamed woods on the best day of a sodden season, I couldn't help looking up through the treetops at the blue patches of sky, hoping to cheat a quick look, to get *my* bird first.

But nothing was happening quickly in this deserted park. Unlike the hectic details of life I had left behind, everything here seemed suspended in the moment of the park's closing for the season. Stained picnic tables dripped melting slush between the boards, and musty fireplaces sticky with ashes and half-burned logs waited to be dredged. Empty swing sets cast still shadows, evoking gray images of children at play. Deer tracks faded into the snowy woods. The only hint of quickness was a rush of woodpeckers rattling industriously at the trees.

The rocky shore was even less animated than the woods. In the middle of the bay, seals lolled belly up on a large, sunny rock, and on a smaller rock rising sharply out of the water, gulls preened, pecked randomly at a dead fish, and nestled in warm crevices. A leaping fish shattered the water's gleaming surface into a Seurat, but it soon recomposed itself. Lobstermen, as if painted for a Down East calendar, rowed fire engine red and navy blue boats among the bobbing trap markers. It was so quiet I heard a seal sneeze.

Idling on a breezy shore, at ease within a picturesque spring panorama of firs and rocks and water, is about as mesmerizing an experience as New England has to offer, but at midterm we still felt some pressure to get our bird and move on.

Frank had lessons to prepare; I had papers to read, and whenever I take those stress profile tests, I always come out type A. (Frank doesn't take the tests, but if he did he would be type B . . . or maybe Z.) The plan was to check off one eagle and go home, but this wasn't as easy as we had hoped. We had to wait, and wait some more. Finally, tired of standing on the shore, we scrambled onto a rough boulder lookout where we ended up staying put for almost two hours.

I had time to count not only the lobster boats but the number of traps each one patrolled. Then, as the boats zigzagged around the bay and the markers bobbed among the sunny ripples, I lost track and started over. "We did take a good long look at that eagle in the zoo," I thought.

I scanned the cloudless sky with my binoculars and repeatedly tried to transform crows and gulls into eagles. I was wishing for a book—*War and Peace*, maybe.

"We could've brought a picnic," I sighed, "but we didn't expect to be here so long, did we?" Looking out over the bay, Frank agreed. I strained to read the company logos on the jets trailing white vapor high over our heads. Without a book, I had to read something. The seals rolled lumpishly into a swim. Yes, it was pretty, but I was thinking about the stack of uncorrected compositions and the midterm exam I still had to make up.

"Wish I'd brought my papers with me," I said.

Frank nodded. "Me too," he said.

I shifted on the craggy rock. "Maybe Sam was wrong about the nests."

"I doubt that," said Frank.

And ten minutes later I said, "Maybe we should get going."

"Not yet," he replied. "We're OK. Let's just wait a little longer."

I remember my surprise when, some time later, a flock of about twenty gulls set up a sharp squawking and flapping from a little evergreen peninsula to our right—the loudest noise since the turnpike. They rushed into the sky in front of us, then darted back above the trees. The crows called up their own forces. They flocked, then dove in unison behind the tall pines. Finally they flushed out what they were all after—a bald eagle gliding steadily before them, rising up, then plunging toward the water.

"There it is!" announced Frank, almost in a whisper, following the eagle's flight with his binoculars. I raised mine and tracked the eagle with him. The din continued until the bird settled on the gulls' rock. With an ominous swagger he forced them one by one into the water, where they floated warily at a distance. I couldn't help thinking of Ben Franklin's preferring the turkey as the national bird, charging the bald eagle with "bad moral character for not getting its living honestly."

The field marks could have been designed by Peterson: white tail feathers, brown body, heavy yellow beak, white head looking like a trick-or-treater's ghost costume. Shrugging off a frenzy of crows, he slowly fluttered his long wing feathers and ruffled them, unperturbed, until the tips crossed neatly over his tail. He eyed the gulls again and strode over the rock to the fish they had hastily left behind. Rip and pause. Slowly he devoured his unearned feast, silvery in the sunlight.

"Satisfied now?" asked Frank, sliding stiffly off the rock. "I think *I* am," he added.

I stayed on the rock, silent, feeling no special urge to check off the bird and run. The bay sparkled. The now familiar boats cruised silently. The five seals watched lazily; the one that had sneezed swam slowly around the rock. The jets streaked white tracks through the cloudless sky. The eagle moved as if in the spotlight. With so much time to take them in, I can see these details sharply to this day. I can summon up the spring breeze; I can hear that sneeze.

Still reluctant to leave, I focused again on this feathered celebrity, most often seen plastered on lecterns, embroidered on flags, lifted high atop public buildings, draped over light switches, and impaled on ye olde colonial rest room signs. This one carried no pewter arrows or plastic olive branches.

This particular eagle may have been a bundle of insecurities, of frustrated dreams, of profound regrets, but to my eyes he seemed sublimely sure of himself, aware of his own symbolic weight. He was in no hurry. Bad actor as this bird might be, I could see why Franklin's turkey lost.

I'm not sure how long it took, but I can remember my arms growing tired from holding the binoculars focused on one spot and my eyes hurting from the glare of the bay that stretched between me and the bird. My time was his time. Frank was the only one who now seemed inclined to leave, and even he shuffled backward toward the trail.

After what seemed an hour, the bird hopped to the middle of the rock, jerked up his head, and lifted off with slow sweeps of his long wings. He rose fast and high over the bay and coasted back over the trees, where the gulls and crows again set up a protest. Then he disappeared. I slipped off the rock and scanned the bay, now darkening into evening. The lobstermen were rowing slowly to shore; I turned back to the woods, hoping another bird would show up so I could stay a little longer.

"Guess we can go now," I said.

As we strolled quietly to the car, the long shadows of the swing set stretched across the snow. Breezes from the bay stirred the pines into a soft whisper.

Back home the next day, my reactions were mixed when I heard that in our absence a rare bald eagle had visited a local pond—about five minutes from our house. I saw that we could have saved some gas and some correcting time, but I also realized that we would have missed the stage setting and the peace that came from giving ourselves the time to see him right.

I've seen many eagles since—in Newfoundland, at Quabbin in Massachusetts, in Alaska—but I still see this first eagle more clearly than any other. This one was entirely our own, as were those workless hours on a sparkling bay in Maine.

Watched by the Birds in India

My first morning in India, I was awakened by *Corvus splendens*. This common crow cawed from our hotel balcony railing and stared directly into our room. Emerging from a jet-lagged slumber, I saw it tip its head curiously and lean forward, ready to wing through the open doors and join us. When Frank jumped up and slammed them shut, the bird settled back, protesting loudly from behind the slightly wavy glass. Accustomed to crows at a distance—winging darkly across a pond, perching on treetops along the highway, lifting off from road-kills—I was surprised at this one's audacity and its apparent plan to come on in. This was only the first of such surprises in India, where I often felt more watched than watching.

We hadn't gone to India to watch birds. Thinking our three weeks visiting major sites in major cities would leave us no time for that, we didn't bring a bird guide or binoculars. We didn't even know where the bird-watching sites were, nor did we plan to find out. What we didn't realize was that we wouldn't need to seek out birds in India. They'd find us. Like the crow on the balcony rail, they were impossible to ignore.

In the cities of India, birds crowd close among the masses of people. On my first outing in Bombay I was both impressed and saddened by the poverty, by the muddy grind of surviving in the monsoon-strafed streets of an overpopulated metropolis. I saw women and children foraging through trash piles for anything of value. And I saw the crows there with them, also foraging.

Truly "common," these birds coasted overhead, perched on trees and buildings, strutted, cawed, and crowded in. I later read that Rudyard Kipling's father had described the birds of India in musical terms, as "a ceaseless *obbligato* accompaniment to all Indian life," and I understood what he meant. These noisy crows were not distant images; they were intimates, adapted to the human goings-on about them. Like all crows, they were wary and alert, but they roamed the streets with disconcerting aplomb, not just skirting the rubbish piles but actively competing. I wondered if Indian nonviolence, or the idea that death may lead to rebirth in other forms, contributed to this toleration, to this willingness to live with them side by side.

Also in Bombay I photographed a flock of common pigeons, usually so easy to pass by. Amid the human crush on the wide plaza at the Gateway of India, an arch of triumph for George V of England, about 150 pigeons hustled and dodged, rapidly devouring a sparse trail of bread crumbs some children scattered for them—a common enough sight. But by the time I got to the Gateway, they had come to seem more symbol than bird. I had pushed my way down grimy streets where bone-thin dogs sidled among the taxis, where teetering sidewalk shelters housed whole families, and where a tiny shrine, beneath the hanging roots of a banyan tree, held a dish of sugar for the ants.

I had passed relays of beggars, so often little girls with babies on their hips. "Please, lady, please?" they said over and over. I had given all the change I had, thus inviting further gentle touches on my arms, further tugs at my skirt, further heartrending bits of begging English. "Help me!" "Just a little?"

At the Gateway, with its snake charmers, its balloon men, its flower vendors, its massive population drifting toward the sea, the feeding pigeons seemed almost self-indulgent, birds faring better than they should, maybe better than the children offering the crumbs. Birds highlighted the great need in this overflowing city. Maybe I was making too much of these common rock pigeons, but in my agitated state of mind it didn't seem so.

In Benares, holiest city of the Hindus and the place where the most devoted go to die, other birds evoked other associations. Here is a place of ritual purification in the Ganges and, should death occur there, a final escape from the cycle of rebirth. The teeming streets ran so heavily with monsoon rain that they seemed tributaries of the swollen river. Barefoot men dragged unsteady rickshaws through the puddles, and drenched white cows passed among the sodden crowds at the market. Shoppers slapped their rumps affectionately.

At the ghats, where wide stone steps reached down to the river, orange-draped holy men sat cross-legged under bamboo umbrellas and worshipers paid homage at a shrine of Ganesha, the elephant-headed son of Siva and Parvati, bedecked in jasmine blossoms. In the churning river young boys frolicked, women submerged themselves slowly, their saris clinging to every contour, and scantily clad men stood quietly, sometimes pressing their hands together in prayer, sometimes offering up wide bowls to the sky.

It was on a damp step of a ghat, sitting near a sign that warned "NOTICE. TAKING OF PHOTOGRAPHY OF BEGGARS, BATHERS, LEPERS AND DEAD BODIES ETC. IS STRICTLY PROHIBITED," that I saw a flock of house sparrows, common at least since the first century A.D. when Pliny named them *Passer domesticus*. Looking in brighter feather than my city sparrows back home, eight of them chirped, splashed, and preened in a Ganges-colored puddle at my feet. In my overcharged mood, they seemed to mimic both the noisy din of the streets behind me and the ritual cleansing at the river.

Like the holy men comfortable on their chosen steps, the sparrows too had their place on the ghats, rarely moving for pedestrians, concentrating on their baths. Not allowed to take pictures of the people and their rituals, I photographed the birds instead, and among my slides they evoke the whole Ganges scene.

Birds were also for me a part of the rich suggestiveness of the countryside—what little I could see from a train window. After an easy night rocking rhythmically in the arms of a sleeper car, I snapped up the window shade and peered through the early morning mist. Here I saw small, mud-splashed settlements, bright green rice paddies and grassland; meandering, brownish streams, cattle grazing and wading hoof deep in mud, tenders gently flicking them with long switches.

And I saw birds among them—crows, of course, and sparrows, but with careful searching, egrets and herons too, standing tall among reedy crops. Emerging from my own dreams, I thought of Krishna dancing with his milkmaids. On that particular morning I saw no *machans*, platforms from which farmers make a racket to protect their crops from birds. At that distance, and in passing, all seemed quiet, soft—the birds in harmony with the fields, the farms, the people, as if sketched by an artist with romantic leanings.

In such a mood I arrived at the Taj Mahal, one of the most romantic of all human monuments. At this elaborate mausoleum built for Mumtaz, favorite wife of the seventeenth-century ruler Shah Jehan, I somehow expected birds—especially peacocks, India's national bird. But what I saw was an occasional crow diving for a drink from a reflecting pool and countless sparrows fluttering in the ornamental shrubs. They contributed little to my experience of the Taj.

It was only at the Red Fort, just down the river, that the birds again stirred imaginings that fit my mood. Site of the shah's palace, it was also the place where he was imprisoned by his son for eight years and died a prisoner. Here were the white marble halls, the elaborate private chambers where the shah spent his captive years, and here was the richly carved and inlaid balcony— Taj-like in its beauty—where he could step outside for an easy view of Mumtaz's monument.

While I was standing in a long line to take my own lattice-work photo of the Taj from this particular balcony, I heard a commotion below, from the precipitous red walls of the fort—parrots, maybe thirty of them, fluttering near the walls, clinging to the ledges. I had read about these birds, kept as cage birds in India and known to be skilled talkers. I also knew that a parrot was the steed of Kama, god of love. Maybe I had read too much medieval literature, too many lays of lovers communicating by messenger birds. Maybe the mobs and the monsoon were getting to me. But I began to wonder if the imprisoned shah too had listened to these chatterers. I wondered if maybe they winged to and from the Taj, delivering love messages to her spirit. Would Kama have ridden one of them on the updrafts?

That night, back at the Taj—softly glowing, otherworldly by moonlight—the messages seemed even more likely, especially when a strong breeze from the direction of the fort rustled through the total quiet of the tomb enclosure.

Not all the birds of India were bearers of romance, however. Some allowed for no dreamy visions, literary or otherwise. Kites, common "pariah kites," cried shrilly from the heights over all beneath them. Sounding more fit for the marshes than for the city streets, they coasted slowly on the updrafts, and when I looked up they gave me again that uneasy sense of being not the watcher but the watched.

I felt this uneasiness too at the Parsi Tower of Silence in Bombay when I noticed the vultures resting heavily in the tall trees. I knew that the Parsis view burial of the dead as unclean, a pollution of mother earth. I knew that they therefore consign their dead to the tower, where they are devoured quickly and cleanly by the vultures. So I also knew the aims of these huge birds. But knowing didn't help my discomfort. I felt uneasy, but at the same time compelled, as so often in India, to see things in unfamiliar ways. These birds of prey were not just another check in my life list, certainly not entertainment or escape; they were a reminder of the complexity of custom, a challenge to my assumptions.

At Benares I was also confronted by such challenges. Constantly moving aside for mourners carrying the shrouded and flower-laden bodies of the deceased to the ghats for ritual cremation and constantly implored by "guides" to witness these smoky rituals close up, I realized that I was unprepared for such square looking at death. My refusals were emphatic, almost panicky. The salesmen seemed to smirk as I backed away.

I didn't escape, though. During an early morning boat ride on the Ganges, I was enjoying the picturesque sight of the worshipers bathing waist deep in the river and even the already smoky ghats, easier to contemplate at a distance. But as I took a picture, I could see a hooded figure out of a medieval morality play move into view and gesture to our rower to come to shore.

As the boat drifted closer to him, my fear rose. I asked our rower to take us back, but he simply stopped rowing, allowing the boat to drift still closer, where the hooded one finally whispered, "Lady! You want some slides of the burning ghats?" and held out a small wrapped package. I shook my head "no" and quickly turned away.

Our rower finally stroked our boat away as I looked with determination across the rushing flow and through the mists to the opposite shore. It was then that I saw the crow, drifting comfortably and rapidly downstream toward us on what appeared to be a log. The rower allowed me not a moment of delusion. "Ah, yes," he announced, reading my mind and calm with certainty. "That's a dead body!" and pulled sharply at the oars, directly toward it. Again I turned away—back to the still-gesturing figure on the shore, back to the smoky pyres. I have read since then that sighting a crow on a dead body floating downriver may be taken as a sign of good luck, but this bird remains a memory of India difficult to transform into good fortune.

My experience with India's birds was random, then, limited to the most common—to those described in the field guides as "a companion of daily life," "most familiar," "man's commensals." I have read about other birds in India, particularly those threatened with extinction for the same bad reasons as in other countries— loss of habitat, sport shooting, destruction by farmers, plume hunting, pesticides, poisons, and of course the press of population. And it is for such reasons that sanctuaries exist there, places where exotic birds thrive and where I would like to go first on my next visit.

But this time I saw only the common birds, uncommonly. They enriched what I saw of Indian life; they challenged me almost daily. Like India itself, they suggested complexity, change, romance, and the shock of the unfamiliar. They invited interpretation. They stimulated thought, feeling, curiosity, as all India did. That crow on the balcony rail was just a foreshadowing.

Ultimates

Coming Back to Capistrano

It's an old picture, a crazed Kodak snapshot from a stack bound with a rubber band, shuffled into an attic desk drawer, discovered . . . and studied. It shows a teenager, neat in a colorful striped cotton dress. She is sitting on a low stone wall, palm open, offering something crumbled to ten indifferent doves. It's the mission church of San Juan Capistrano, more than twenty-five years ago—a moment stopped by the camera and luring me back like the swallows.

I extracted that picture from the deck, returning the others to my mother's attic, and for a few more years it sat on my desk, working its way to the bottom of my "To Do" box with the unanswered letters and the abandoned diary. It stayed there until a midwinter academic conference was scheduled so near to Capistrano that I couldn't resist a return trip. I'm not sure what I was looking for, especially at that time of year; I knew the famous swallows were still wintering far south of the sanctuary arch.

I think I was hoping for a pleasant evocation of those traveling years with my parents and my younger sister, those annual transcontinental car trips—seeing the United States in our big tail-finned De Soto. My family probably went to Capistrano in the first place at least partly because of the Leon René song "When the Swallows Come Back to Capistrano." We went to look for those swallows (and, I would guess, to see the mission founded by Father Junípero Serra, a hero of my religion classes). This time the "come back" part seemed like a command, a promise of almost certain nostalgia, a twinge of heartache for a childhood long past. I took the photograph with me; I think I was also looking for that teenager, the skinny adolescent ignored by the doves.

Entering the grounds with my ticket in hand, I was at first surprised by how familiar the place looked: the high surrounding walls, the greens and golds of trees and flowers, the stone paths, the four bells, and particularly the high ruin of the arch where the swallows nest. Missing was the summer tourist crowd gathered before the arch, watching the swallows soar and flutter, perch on and lift off the narrow ledges. Missing were the swallows.

After a stroll around the grounds, in a warmth made even more comforting by contrast with the blizzard I had left at home, I discovered a low stone wall much like the one in the picture— minus doves—and sat down. I would deliberately recall those years. The quiet helped clear my mind's flight back.

What first came to mind was not swallows at all, but those annual vacations. Bored with the two-by-four beach at New Hampshire's Lake Winnipesaukee and the pinball games at the Weirs, we all longed for more. So for ten years straight we took marathon drives, following green-highlighted roads on AAA maps as far west from New England as we could get. When my father's job allowed two weeks of vacation, we got only to Mount Rushmore, Yellowstone, or the Grand Canyon. But when he was promoted to three weeks off, then four, the Pacific beckoned to us as to the original settlers. "California, here we come," my father would sing off-key and lean harder on the accelerator, driving many late afternoons into the blinding setting sun.

We got lost among the mining towns of West Virginia, slogged through muddy midwestern cow pastures when the AAA-marked route flooded out, drove into atomic-looking thunderheads, and pulled off the road when hailstones pounded a rough staccato on the roof. Row after tedious row of cornstalks flashed tightly into view, fanned out in ruler-straight regiments to the horizon, and closed up again. Sequences of Burma Shave signs broke the monotony:

> *SHE WISHED TO BE HELD*
> *SHE GAVE A WHISTLE*
> *BUT SHE WAS REPELLED*
> *BY HIS AWFUL BRISTLE.*
> *BURMA SHAVE!*

At tourist stops, boys wired advertisements to our bumpers, sometimes right over the ones we had acquired two or five states back: "Visit Jesse James Cave!" "Come to the Donkey Derby Days!" "Goin' to Cripple Creek!" "We got our kicks on Route 66!" I can remember hypnotically counting segments of the broken white center line to beyond a thousand, and I think I could draw the orange-and-black, black-and-orange billboards for the competing caverns—Onondaga and Meramec—including the final gasp at the jug handle, allowing an immediate return, YOU HAVE JUST PASSED ONONDAGA CAVERNS—TURN HERE! I don't remember complaining. They might have been five hundred, even six hundred mile days, but they were an adventure, planned for, anticipated, shared, cherished—and in any case far superior to pinball.

Sometimes, to get out of the stiff wind coming through the car's open windows, I would make a hideout on the floor, tucking one end of a blanket over the woven cord on the back of my mother's seat and wedging the other end taut into the crevice of the backseat. Here, by flashlight, I could read my Uncle Scrooge McDuck funny books and, in later years, the agonies of Jane Eyre or the legal entanglements of Dickens's Jarndyce and Jarndyce.

At breakfast in diners I played crashing jukebox rock and roll and then coaxed my mother to turn it on in the car. With my father rocketing down the Oklahoma Turnpike at close to eighty miles an hour, she didn't share my delight in the real-life accident sound effects or the lyrics, "Transfusion! Transfusion! . . . my red corpsuckles are in mass confusion!" But I didn't like the incessant hum of the tires without Nervous Novice, the Platters, or Elvis, "Weee . . . el, since mah baby lef' me."

At ease behind the wheel of his always-new car, my father drove, except for minor interruptions for lunches, souvenirs, ladies' rooms, mines, and caves—until the 4:30 P.M. negotiations: "Let's stop now; it's getting late" followed by "No, let's go on a little longer." This was usually the time when my sister, rested from sleeping most of the day's miles across the continent, would stake her claim to a pool, and I would make my case for a TV. And finally, at 6:00 or 7:00 in the evening, exhausted, he would succumb.

"I don't want to *buy* the place!" he would complain to the manager as the screen door slammed behind him. "I just want to *sleep* here!" he would predictably grumble as he got back behind the wheel at various rejected motels, hotels, and cabins, still determined to search, often too late, for clean beds, a pool, a TV, and a bargain. Headin' west.

Sitting on that wall, I wished they were all with me. They could have helped me recall that particular crossing into California, the time we went to Capistrano. I could remember getting up in the dark, in the coolness of the Las Vegas predawn, and setting off into the desert. I could remember the canvas water bag tied to the De Soto's grille and, balanced out the window, the little ice water–filled air-conditioner canister, guaranteed to transform the desert heat of the car into "comforting coolness." By noon the water in the canister had cooked the air to the temperature of the desert, and no matter how often we tugged at the little venetian blind cord meant to open the vents, the car got hotter and hotter. Not wanting to waste time refilling the canister, we endured, like Gold Rush prospectors, waiting for the relief of the steep climb over the Rockies and down into California.

Memories flocked. Like the swallows coming back, they struggled to take hold, displacing one another—vigorous and alive. Sitting on that wall, glancing occasionally at the picture in my hand, I felt more there than here. I wouldn't have been shocked to see my mother aiming her boxy Brownie camera at me.

Still in the company of that earlier self, I got up and walked beneath the shaded arch, silent in the winter sun, and tried to think about the swallows. I remembered their busily nesting flocks peering down from their perches at the tourists peering up. I remembered being happy they were there, just where they were supposed to be, a feeling I have had many times since: when I heard people in Paris say *merci;* when I watched Venetians guide upholstered gondolas down shady canals; when I photographed

Queen Elizabeth, looking a lot like the queen on the pound notes in my pocket.

It probably was a "God's in his heaven / All's right with the world" feeling, and maybe in those very words, since I had to recite Browning's "The Year's at the Spring" every year from first grade to graduation. I took pictures of those swallows, I remembered, tiny black spots against the gold, but they were pictures long lost.

I've learned since about the swallows' cosmopolitan ways, their thousands of miles of migration to the south and then back, their aerodynamic design ideal for catching insects on the wing, their storied annual arrival at Capistrano on March 19, punctual harbingers of spring. I can see now that my father had something in common with them: their endurance. But what that teenager in the picture saw eluded me.

I couldn't ignore her presence, her influence on the place before my eyes, but she seemed both an intimate and a stranger. I even began to wonder if I was creating her more from hindsight than from any true memory. I wondered what she might have been thinking, feeling. Was she enjoying the calmness there before the sanctuary arch? Did she have any premonitions of the disruptions of the teen years, the slow alienation from those annual trips . . . and, at times, even from her parents? It was charming to think that maybe she noticed the fledging flights of the young swallows and thought of her own initiations, but more likely she hadn't even noticed there were young swallows at all.

Like March swallows in Mexico, she was probably thinking of someplace else. Capistrano, I remembered, was the turning point, that journey moment now so familiar to me when a traveler's thoughts are in two places at once. Maybe she felt suspended between those worlds, wanting to linger in California but also drawn across the thousands of miles to Massachusetts. She probably liked Capistrano well enough, but I'll bet she was also thinking about her cocker spaniel and her boyfriend back home.

I look back on both of those visits, from the vantage point of my desk where I am now, several years later, trying to write about them. What emerges is a compelling awareness of the passage of time and of a simultaneous desire to stop the reel somehow, to freeze a single frame. I felt then, and I feel now, the need to think about time itself. Two similar occasions, both from earlier days, come suddenly to mind.

One involves my best girlfriend and me, both about twelve. For several years we had been good friends, and we made constant vows to remain loyal. Once we even planned to declare our sisterhood by piercing our fingers and merging blood as we had seen in the cowboy and Indian movies. Sterilized common pin at the ready, we both decided that our vow itself meant more than any foolish ritual and agreed to wait for some lucky chance when we would both get cuts at the same time.

When we were not running a bogus telephone quiz show ("Who wrote *The Three Musketeers?*") or asking shopkeepers giggling questions ("Do you have Prince Albert in a can?" "Is your freezer running?") we talked often that summer about the passing of time. I'm not sure why we were so time conscious then, but it occurs to me now that we were both just weeks short of becoming teenagers, a transition probably much on our minds. I remember one morning in particular when, running across an open field, we stopped, breathless, near an apple tree. I remember our waving at the air behind us, then shouting in prearranged unison, "Good-bye to our past! Good-bye!" I also remember that she added, "We'll never see you again" and then ran on ahead of me. Two summers later she moved the untraversable distance of two towns away, enough for us to lose our sisterhood forever.

On another occasion I was waiting alone for an overdue trolley in a Boston subway station. Fast approaching my twenty-first birthday, I felt old and vulnerable. Without humor, and with no reference to the transportation system, I thought of myself aging as I stood there and of the grim fact that I would never again be as young as I had been just the moment before. That particular time could never come back, I mused, getting sadder by the minute. Progress toward death was inevitable and relentless. Would I ever be happy again? Would I ever be free of that taunting awareness of time's slipping away? I was relieved when the trolley clattered in to deliver me to college.

Ironically, and for whatever reasons—being too busy for such momentous pauses, a more mature compromise with the facts of life, fear of looking too closely at the clock—these experiences have become rarer with the passing of time. Except for the undeniable urge to climb the steeple and choke the clapper as the midnight bells at Verona tolled out my twenty-ninth year, I have rarely since focused so self-consciously on time as I did on that second visit to Capistrano . . . and as I am doing now.

Sitting here at my desk, I am aware of how hard it is to take such long views, of how impossible it is to recapture a past long gone. Even on location, what I recalled were pieces of experience, snippets of emotion, vague visual impressions informed by a snapshot—like swallows on the wing. And I couldn't be sure how accurate these tiny recollections really were. T. S. Eliot's elusive "These are hints and guesses, / Hints followed by guesses" seemed a perfect expression of my dilemma. I had gone to Capistrano that winter to recreate something of my own past, perhaps to make some connections with my present self, but my success was slight.

I enjoyed remembering those vacations, I appreciated visiting Father Serra's old monastery again, and I liked populating the sanctuary arch with visions of long-gone swallows—a charming twinge of nostalgia after all—but I kept thinking there was more to know. I was sure of it.

So almost immediately after my return from Capistrano, I placed that well-traveled photograph on the kitchen table and quizzed my parents about *their* Capistrano memories.

"Yes, it was a beautiful day," said my mother, "and wasn't that an awfully pretty dress?"

"Yes," I replied a bit impatiently, eager to get to the heart of the matter, "it was."

She tipped the photograph to the light. "You look good with your hair short."

Watching her finger the photograph that she herself had taken, I remembered *she* was the one most bored with the two-by-four beach (or any size beach) and the pinball games. She was the one who inspired, shopped for, packed up, mapped out, and orchestrated those transcontinental trips. My father set the big goals, earned the money, and covered the miles; she did the groundwork.

"Remember that day, Jim?" she asked, handing the picture to my father.

"Yup, it was a nice place. I remember it was hot . . . damned hot," he answered, laying the picture on the kitchen table. "Lots of tourists, lots of birds."

"I think we headed back to Vegas from there," he went on. For my father, all roads worth their tarmac headed back to Vegas.

"Stayed in some godforsaken mountain pass that night. Remember?" he asked my mother.

"The one with the snakes?" she responded immediately.

"That's the one! The cabin with the broken window in the bedroom and the water snakes along the river right behind the place. Remember you didn't sleep a wink that whole night?" He laughed.

As he talked, I was reminded of the long drives he did as the sole driver, and I wondered what it had been like trying to keep us all happy. As he traced his own mental road map to specific mines, caves, and souvenir shops, I was impressed with how well he knew those desert roads, route numbers, mountain passes, entrances, and exits—headin' west, then east. He's the one who got us all to Onondaga and Meramec, to Jesse James's hideout, to Cripple Creek, to the casinos in Las Vegas—over the years, to just about every stop along the way.

"Remember you and Marie always wanted a ladies' room right *after* we left the gas station?"

Yes, I remembered. I also remembered a time shared with both of them and with my sister, who couldn't recall Capistrano at all but who reminds me periodically about a particular motel pool in Vegas where I convinced her of the delights of the deep end. She lost her grip on the side, panicked, and had to be rescued. I remembered my father edging the De Soto around the treacherous curves of that mountain pass, a narrow sandy trail with no railings, open only in the summer. I had loved leaning out the car window and looking down the precipice. I remembered the moon-shaped indentations impressed deep in my mother's palms as she nervously clenched her fists.

I remembered more about all of them than I did about that teenager trying to feed the doves. Our recollections were random, it seemed, and very much our own. That teenager at Capistrano was clearly gone, just a single moment out of a million memories—my moment—and not so clear at that.

Only as I write this now do I realize that just six months after our conversation over the kitchen table my father died—suddenly and too young—and Capistrano has thus become, even more indelibly than before, associated with time and loss in my life. I will cover no more miles with him, skirt no more precipices, demand no more ladies' rooms, ask no more questions about itineraries, learn no more about how all those miles felt to him. No more.

More and more, those times elude me. Nostalgia, *with* the pain.

I would like to go to Capistrano again. I'd like to take my children there, to form their own impressions, maybe to take a picture, to update some memories. I'd like them to see the swallows as I did, for the annual return to the high sanctuary arch seems now not just an arrival by a flock of punctual birds but a harbinger of real hope—for springtime, for renewal, for an ultimate order in things, for filling again a space that seems so permanently empty. They mean more now than they did then.

The Attractions of Ukpik

At first I dismissed him as a snowy piling frozen into the desolate beach. But when the yellow eyes stared unblinking back at me I realized I had finally come upon my first snowy owl. Only twenty yards away, on a bright January afternoon, he stayed put and gave me time to say "he" with confidence, his pure whiteness unmarked by the female's telltale breast bars. Every once in a while he would swivel his head toward the frosted dune grass or deliberately lift his feathery feet and fan his claws stiffly; but mostly he just sat still, his upper eyelids settling over a disdainful glare.

Later, owl fashion among my library books, it was easy to learn more about the snowy because this remarkable "ermine bird," being white, large, and comfortable in daylight, has been studied by many. It has commanded attention, invited narrative, stirred speculation.

Observers report on the snowies' circumpolar range, their adaptations to the arctic freeze, and their fondness for perching on small protuberances, or *pingaluks*, in the tundra. They describe courtship flights, egg laying in timed sequence, domestic arrangements, and even lowered birthrates when the food supply is low. Like the killdeer, snowies resort to a wounded-bird charade to protect their young, but in spite of careful guarding, many owlets do not survive the rigors of their birthplace. And in the research they make identifying noises like *krow-ow* and *krohgogogok*. One Alaskan listener works by analogy to capture their sounds: "He barks like sled dog sometimes; sometimes he makes call like tu-lu-lok," that is, like a raven.

Other observers report snowies' taste for ptarmigans and arctic hares, but especially their reliance on lemmings, those small rodents whose crashes in population force snowies to travel farther afield for food in "irruptions," or large-scale invasions. In 1926 they irrupted as far south as North Carolina and hitched rides on southerly seagoing ships. One hungry young snowy is reported to have flown 3,500 miles from Canada to Russia.

But these birds have inspired more than ornithological reports. They have also led private lives, lives of a less scientific sort, that stir the imagination.

Among Paleolithic populations, the snowy seems to have had magical significance. In fact the first identifiable representation of birds of any sort is of a family of snowies at the Cave of Les Trois Frères in southern France. Probably forced south by the glacier (or a food shortage), these ancient birds stare back with the unblinking focus of my first snowy and remind me of my own compulsion to take notice of the event.

In our time too, the beauty of the snowy is tempting to artists, not so much for magical purposes as out of delight in such pristine perfection. It's a rare cold-zone gift shop or art gallery that doesn't display at least one drawn, painted, or carved snowy owl. Snowies are sketched on pillows and pins, painted on lampshades, woven into rugs, photographed for postcards, displayed on over-size posters.

At the National Gallery in Washington, Audubon's snowy pair perches high in a tree, backlit by the moon, almost fluores-cent. The snowy is an easy temptation to an artist, a subject with automatic points of perfection and likely to be appreciated by an audience.

Ironically, this luminescent beauty makes real life even more difficult for the owls. Prominent among the early accounts of migrations are taxidermists' totals, like those of E. S. Cameron, who reports calmly that in 1907 he "had five hundred sent to him for preservation." Edward Howe Forbush himself, natural historian and admirer of all American birds, tells of stalking an elusive snowy and then concedes, with disarming appreciation, "Twice I have had her within easy gunshot, but had I killed her I would have missed her reception of the Crows and that eery following of that unknown form across that cloudless sky." He's glad he missed that one.

Reports of sightings, especially in the past, sometimes end with a jolt, as in the description of a dilatory snowy that by July 15 had yet to return north: "The previous week had been extremely hot, and the bird is conjectured to have lived in a large ice house nearby, upon the cupola of which it was shot," goes the account. Even sadder, such destruction seems not to be safely relegated to the past; some hunters still see snowies as targets, more appealing stuffed than on the wing. The snowy trophy.

Delight in the beauty of the owl is not universal, however, at least not in one Alaskan poem about how a snowy might look from a ptarmigan's point of view. Maybe forgetting his usual habit of din-ing on ptarmigans, and proud of his great white gorgeousness, this poetic snowy has the temerity to pay suit to one of them but is predictably rejected. She then mocks him with a litany of abuses:

Ukpik, go away!
With your big head
And your too large eyes
And your sorry-looking legs—
You are ugly!
Who would want you for a husband?
. . .
You big dumpy owl,
With no feet and no neck!

No sleeping with the enemy for this ptarmigan, and so the spurned suitor heads back to his pingaluk.

Depending on the observer, snowies may also be seen as embodiments of terror, "white ghosts" with "savage" or "tigerish" glares, their calls heard with trepidation, as in Thomas Nuttall's somewhat overwrought account describing the call of the snowy as the "unearthly ban of Cerberus; and heard amidst a region of cheerless solitude, his lonely voice augments rather than relieves the horrors of the scene."

Among the natives of the icebound north, with whom Ukpik lives in close proximity, the fear is sometimes expressed in tales, as in one where the owl violently kills not only a wolf but the wolf's mate and their two cubs, or in the story of the red-eyed Ukpik that is kept from killing off a whole village only by the protective magic of a poor boy.

In a 1940s true-life ghost story, Sydney A. Montague brags of killing a snowy on Akpatok Island, much feared by Eskimos. But as he proudly carries his prey to his boat, he stumbles upon an ancient human burial ground littered with bones and skulls: "I felt myself shiver, and kept turning my head with a strange feeling that there was something behind me." It isn't until he has rowed safely offshore that he realizes his dead snowy is still on the island . . . back with the bones.

It is also common to impute human traits to snowies. "Ukpik just doesn't look quite bright," says one naturalist, calling attention to his rather "sappy, fatuous stare," but a Micmac legend sees more admirable human traits. In this story the bird laments the loss of the golden age at the time when the irritated god Glooscap withdraws his favor from the animals because of their perpetual quarreling. "Koo, koo, shoos," says the wise and mournful snowy, "I am sorry."

In Eskimo fables too they often play roles more human than owlish. In one didactic tale, wisdom prevails as an overly emotional, silly, dancing snowy is easily outsmarted by a smaller but more clever "shik-shik," or ground squirrel. In another an inattentive snowy, having snagged one hare with each claw, is rushed headlong into a boulder, cartoon fashion, when his scurrying prey separate and run, one on each side of the rock. "The story means you should watch where you are going," offered one Eskimo explicator. In another tale, "The Mountain Called Aiyassiruk," the snowy is the clever one, metamorphosing from man to bird and back again, meanwhile building up a store of winter food for his hungry family.

For me the snowy embodies the icy north where I've spent practically every winter of my life. The bird suggests not the sparkling distractions of Christmas or the consoling promise of spring, but the absolute, iced-in grasp of winter—the sudden, breathtaking chill of stepping out the front door, the snowbanks too high to pile higher, the cruel seizing at the heart when the car slips into a skid.

Most often struggling on the far edge of survival in the polar regions, the snowy that I see on our own temporarily frozen promontories brings me notice of a world relentlessly colder than mine. Alert when all else seems frozen dead, at home in places I gladly relinquish to the ice, the snowy reminds me of a place shared with arctic foxes, ivory gulls, snow geese, polar bears, and other populations necessarily more rugged than I am. Snowies remind me of what's going on up there and make me a little more tolerant of our snowflakes and far more pleased with our spring.

Nearly every year since that first one, I have tried to see a snowy owl. For the search, I myself must migrate, moving out of my own winter shelters and closer to the desolation that snowies prefer. One year I discover a snowy on a windy rock in a storm-darkened ocean harbor. Another year I watch one hunting from a frozen tuft of dune grass at the beach, and still another year, with binoculars, I find one at a great distance, buffeted on top of a weathered shed in an icy meadow. I'm so cold in the wind I can barely stay to bring the bird into focus. But stay I do.

I enjoy this annual search for a snowy, and because it's rarely easy to find one, I appreciate the reward all the more. Maybe it's also the special attraction to what's difficult, here in what Lord Byron called the "moral" north.

The Featherless Bipeds and the Birds

I n his *Biophilia*, naturalist E. O. Wilson warns:

> *The one process going on now that will take millions of years to correct is the loss of genetic and species diversity by the destruction of natural habitats. This is the folly our descendants are least likely to forgive.*

Bill McKibben titles an entire volume *The End of Nature*, and Leonard Lutwack, author of *Birds in Literature*, warns that "it is no longer possible to save large enough tracts to make any difference to endangered species," concluding that "learning to deal with a diminished world is our inevitable lot." On a more cosmic scale, Lewis Thomas's late-night thoughts include a grim premonition of total emptiness after nature's dying is done: "I cannot listen to the last movement of the Mahler Ninth without the door-smashing intrusion of a huge new thought: death everywhere, the dying of everything, the end of humanity."

Assessments like these, expressing varying degrees of sadness, alarm, resignation, and misery, become increasingly impossible to ignore. It is no longer easy simply to admire the birds, to find consolation in their predictable presence, reassurance in the evidence of "Godes plentee," as Chaucer saw them, or inspiration at our beck and call. Appreciation is now accompanied by an inevitable fear about the future of the birds, and ultimately of ourselves. It hasn't always been so.

In my own reading in the literature of the past, I continually come upon the birds, those living abundantly close to the human lives around them as they bestow fertility, assist at births, guide people to food and shelter, predict the weather, warn of the turns of personal destiny, deliver good or bad luck, help with the hunt, bear messages, provide transportation, and teach lessons about generosity or pride or foolishness or love.

I cheer for the Ojibwa birds that play ball with the north wind and lose, condemning themselves to a long migration south every year. I admire the resourcefulness of European storks that seek out the moon as a winter resort, and I envy the fabulous phoenix that every five hundred years arises reborn from its own ashes. I yearn for the medieval *caladrius* that visits the sick, absorbs their ailments by engaging them in a staring match, then carries the sickness off to the clouds. And I am grateful to the robin who, Antigone-like, covers the human corpse with leaves while it awaits proper burial.

In reading, too, I discover something of the complexity in a particular species. A Zoroastrian's virtuous raven who cleanses the earth of carrion is a Muslim's devil raven, guilty of devouring unclean refuse; but the raven may also be a Norseman's bird-god, an Alaskan's clever trickster, or a Cornishman's King Arthur awaiting reincarnation. One peacock may be the embodiment of human pomposity, a strutting show-off poised for a fall; another may be the worthy bird of Hera, with tail feathers bearing the hundred eyes of her beloved Argos, who died loyally serving her. The wise old owl of Athena may also be India's bird of ill omen or a European warning of bad things to come, with its "hollow hootings, fearful shrieks, serpent-like hissings and coffin-maker snappings."

In the past I easily discover direct, personal relationships between birds and people—Solomon conversing with the hoopoe, the cock, and the peewit; Saint Francis counting the birds among his family members, along with Brother Sun and Sister Moon; Arab tribes fighting off the Abyssinians with the help of benevolent swallows that drop stones on the invaders' heads.

Through augury, or listening to "bird talk," ancient fortune-tellers translate the messages of the birds, while the *auspex* or bird-watcher reads significance in their actions, their bones, their entrails; hence the good or bad auspices that still hover over our futures. Breaking the Thanksgiving turkey's wishbone, a part of us still hopes for a premonition of joy.

Sometimes, and even more intimately, actual transformations occur, with humans metamorphosing into birds, like Ovid's Alcyone changed into the calming halcyon bird of the sea, or the European millers transformed into cuckoos because they refused bread to a starving Christ, or the dead sailors reanimated into storm petrels. Hybrids partake of both identities—the human-headed, irritating winged harpies that snatch food from the banquet tables or the more benevolent falcon-headed Horus, who protects the pharaohs.

The writing of the past also reveals our persistent yearning to be like the birds. Young Icarus, foolhardy with his own new wings, flies too near to the sun, which melts the wax attaching them to his back so that he falls into the sea and drowns. The souls of the dead commonly fly birdlike to heaven, and even Zeus temporarily becomes a swan.

Leonardo da Vinci designs flying machines, ancestors of the ones now winging us around the world or launching some of us to the moon where those storks used to winter. Pythagoras himself is said to have once been a peacock.

Evocations of birds abound, nesting and flying, posing and preening in countless manuscripts and carvings, paintings and pediments, totems and masks. They weave in and out of fabrics, ornament drapes and dresses, and shape themselves into urns, candelabras, ewers, gargoyles, and waterspouts. Chaucer's bird parliament is so crowded he can barely find a place to squeeze in:

> *That erthe and air and tree and every lake*
> *So ful was that unnethe [scarcely] was there space*
> *For me to stonde, so ful was al the place.*

Eagles hover symbolically over Saint John and his gospel, and in hundreds of renditions the Christ child caresses a pet bird as he is cradled in his mother's lap. In one medieval illumination, while the courtly lady makes eyes at her knight, their two horses gaze longingly at one another, as do their two pet birds, similarly smitten. Birds sing in symphonies and operas, in country ditties and hard rock.

Among the images of the past, it is easy to discover a plenitude of birds. Recently, during a casual afternoon in a late Renaissance gallery, I found the Christ child with his pet bird, many glowing doves of the Holy Spirit, and Noah's reconnaissance bird. With closer searching I discovered a caged bird on Saint Jerome's shelf, also contemplative as the saint ponders the afterlife. I spotted a fat partridge among the many animals at John the Baptist's rushing stream, a fruitful nature's approval of his mission, and I found Christ himself, enveloped in six red wings, rising above his crucifixion, a simultaneous evocation of both his humanity and his divinity. Birds both decorate and reinforce the symbolic messages of the artwork.

It is sometimes disheartening to see that, even with a long catalog of intimacy, often affection, between birds and humans there may also be found both insensitivity and cruelty, not only in the ancient dissecting of birds to discover omens for the future, but also in the cutting out of tongues, the clipping of wings, the crucifying, the plucking, and the pulverizing.

In the past, however, assumptions about the abundance of the birds and their overall subordinate place in the pecking order, insensitive as they may have been, were less cause for alarm than they are today. Flocks by the millions continued to block out the moon, while augurs and *auspexes*, farmers and rain dancers, had little lasting effect on the totals. Even in this century, Theodore Roethke could write of a "delirium of birds" discovered near his house.

But now things are different. Without sliding into the millennialist slough of despond, it is nevertheless important to notice that we are breaking the ties that have bound the birds and us together since our earliest gasps of appreciation—when we first encountered snowy owls staring back at us or envied hunting birds capturing their prey, then portrayed them on cave walls. One sad example: the overall population of some migratory songbirds appears to have dropped by half in just the past twenty years. Other ominous patterns are all too easy to find. How silent might our springs become?

The plenitude of the living record suggests that for the entire span of human existence the birds have been there with us—sources of delight, stimulations to our imaginations, symbolic embodiments of our highest yearnings. In awe, Shelley grants the skylark supremacy in song and settles for just *half* the bird's gladness to provide inspiration for his own poem. The birds have also been allies, companions, intimates of our most private feelings.

And now, more from neglect than from malice, we are destroying their habitat, withdrawing our protection, and ignoring the consequences as we allow losses unlike any others in history. In Hitchcock's world, the birds strike back in their own defense, but that is movie myth based in fiction. The delirium of real birds seems to be done.

Would that they could speak to the Solomon in all of us, crowd in on us again, demand our attention, as they did so often in the past. Would that more of us were like the patient Saint Kevin of Seamus Heaney's poem, who nurtured nesting blackbirds in the palm of his outstretched hand until they could fly away:

> *Kevin feels the warm eggs, the small breast, the tucked*
> *Neat head and claws and, finding himself linked*
> *Into the network of eternal life,*
>
> *Is moved to pity: now he must hold his hand*
> *Like a branch out in the sun and rain for weeks*
> *Until the young are hatched and fledged and flown.*

Lacking Kevin's love, would that all the birds could be phoenixes.

Bird-Watching . . . in Italy?

In my years of reading, teaching, and traveling I had encountered many Italian birds, both living and not: courageous birds over Lake Avernus, the toxic entrance to the Underworld where no birds fly safely; gracious peacocks in Pompeiian frescoes; mosaic birds at Saint Mark's in Venice; multitudes of birds in frescoes, statues, and mass cards picturing Saint Francis; birds ornamenting the saint himself from head to foot; symbolic birds in Dante's *Divine Comedy*, vivid images of sin or salvation, winging their way to hell or paradise. Dante was a bird-watcher.

So it seemed only right that bird-watching be among the many ventures planned for another sabbatical year, this time in Italy. We'd read, write, revise class notes, visit museums and galleries, spend time with the kids, and track down some more of those world-famous birds.

I wasn't even discouraged when it took a month longer than scheduled for our car to arrive on a slow boat to Genoa, nor did I lose faith as we visited and rejected first a series of dilapidated digs too far below our dreams, then luxurious condominiums way beyond our means. And when we finally drove our own car up to a villa for rent high in the Tuscan hills, only an hour's drive from Florence, a surprisingly affordable villa with huge rooms, marble floors, a walk-in fireplace, and long country views on every side, I was sure our plans were all *in via*.

I was all the more certain when, soon after we paid our security deposit and our first month's rent, sparrows began landing on our balcony rail, where we had placed some bread crumbs. From that same balcony, as I hung out the late summer laundry, I could make out less familiar birds in the distance, fluttering about the tall, pointed cypresses. We made plans to hike there, with binoculars. Idyllic.

Idyllic, that is, until the autumn sent a chill through the cavernous rooms and a windy rainstorm forced open the balcony doors and soaked the marble floor of our *salotto*. I thought someone had broken in. The fireplace, plus the sparse and costly heating, offered little comfort as I padded throughout the night to pull the covers over the kids. Even less charming were the unwelcome salvos of gunfire that woke us all at dawn. Soon after the fireworks started, our hilltop neighbors, already widely scattered and remote, began to move out. Windows were boarded up, doors permanently shut, entrance gates padlocked.

Still enchanted, however, and determined to make the most of this liberating year, we adjusted our budget for bigger heating bills, stacked the beds with comforters, and set out to look for birds along the nearby trails.

We rarely saw a bird. As we passed the closed-up villas, red VIETATO signs ordered us to keep our distance. Seeming more common than pinecones, multicolored shotgun shells littered the trail. And soon after, we learned that this was the usual closing time for our own villa. No one had ever spent a whole winter there. The fireplace was for family Christmas visits—Tuscan atmosphere *di Natale*—not for winter residence.

When the autumn winds got colder, the heating bills reached the height of the cypresses, and the picturesque hour's drive down to Florence threatened to become a precarious slide. When we finally admitted we were worried about the gunfire on those bird-watching trails, we began to wonder if it wasn't time for us to move also. By then we were able to read the signs advising tire chains, and I took special notice of the torn and dented guardrails along the steep road.

But we didn't begin to pack until one evening when I focused my binoculars from the balcony rail across to the cypresses, trying to bring in a distant and very busy bird. What I got was not the bird, but a hunter and his dog stalking the cypress where my bird had unwisely perched. The hunters can have their hills, I thought. I saw him shoot, but I didn't stay to admire his aim. We decided to sacrifice our deposit to the greedy landlord, move within the city limits, and retire our car.

I knew we would have to work a little harder for our live birds, but the birds in the Florentine galleries and chapels would be that much closer, and not long after we arrived in town I made a plan to visit the Fiera degli Uccelli—the Festival of the Birds— at the city's old Porta Romana. How nice, I remember thinking, an entire daylong festival in honor of the birds. Sort of a craft fair with feathers. Maybe I would meet some fellow bird-watchers there; maybe I'd pick up a few pointers for the best places to look.

Busy with morning chores, I got there late, as many of the exhibitors were packing up to leave. The day was dreary, the park grimy and dusty, the battered metal cages stacked and shoved roughly against one another. Inside these cages were crowded various birds, most of them unfamiliar to me, and along the aisles were tables well stocked with equipment for the hunt—guns, bullets, camouflage clothing, boots, nets, cages, decoys, and other tools of the trade, also unfamiliar to me. No bird tea cozies here. This was not a jolly scene. The exhibitors looked menacing, and no one beckoned me over for a closer look. In fact if I lingered too long at one of the caged birds, they heaved it, squawking and chattering, all the more quickly to the van. I realized later that I must have looked too much like a bird-watcher, not among the hunters' favorites in Italy.

This was only the first of many revelations. It didn't take me long to realize just how pervasive is the Italian passion for the hunt . . . and the Italian taste for eating wild birds. I began to notice butcher shop posters for fresh *passerotti,* an ironically affectionate term for dinner sparrows. Inside the shops I discovered rows of tiny birds on display, lined up for *spiedini,* ready for the spit. Sometimes they were camouflaged under tinselly red or green sprigs of fake parsley, but I became an expert at finding them in the cases. I noticed that rural restaurant menus proudly featured birds of the *caccia*—the hunt—for dinner specials, and even toys were connected to the *caccia.*

In one shopwindow, among the Legos and the Ravensburger nature puzzles, was displayed a tall frame with whirling plastic pigeons for targets and a popgun for bringing them down. One night I watched a television quiz show give prizes to the person best able to recite the opening and closing dates of the hunting season. "Blackbird! September 21 to December 31!" shouted one well-fed contestant. "Jackdaw! September 21 to February 28!" countered the other, also rotund.

It was fast becoming obvious that for many Italians hunting birds is simply one rather pleasant aspect of daily life. Hunters stalk the trails among the abandoned villas. Cooks skewer up their *spiedini*. Families dine grandly on wild birds. For many Italians, hunting dinner birds is as natural as boiling up the gnocchi.

But it was also becoming obvious to me that not all Italians feel the same about the birds. On the evening news, for example, I followed the court case of popular actor and singer Adriano Celentano, who, in a TV monologue, vigorously criticized the Italian devotion to hunting. "There are about two million hunters in Italy who annually conduct a massacre, killing two billion birds," he said. He then went on to advise his cheering audience and his many viewers to write a sentence at the bottom of an upcoming referendum ballot—"Hunting is against love." For publicly recommending defacement of ballots, thereby making them invalid, this celebrity was threatened with a two-year jail sentence. I watched for news reports of his progress, and on the day the judge dismissed all charges, I found myself smiling at the television.

About this time, too, I began to explore the bird-watching magazines, where I discovered further efforts to stir sympathy for the ever pursued birds.

"Where the Italians live, the birds don't," announced one article. "The smart birds avoid Italy altogether, and the others learn to stay very, very quiet," proclaimed another. I read of complaints against hunters at Assisi whose irritating gunfire punctuated local ceremonies in honor of the saint who considered birds his siblings.

Photographs showed birds grimly strangled in mazes of netting, birds peering out the tiny holes of shipping crates, huge hunting parties setting off for a sunny afternoon's recreational shoot. One close-up was of a dead kestrel with wings stretched wide, hanging gruesomely from a crude cross—evidently someone's joke. These images were having the intended effect on me. I admit I have never been an admirer of hunting, and I have been accused of harboring a Bambi complex because I fail to see the pleasure in killing a deer caught in the crosshairs of a telescopic sight or, worse, wounding it with a bow and arrow. (I also admit to being influenced by a real Maine hunter who felt nothing but disdain for the Boston city slickers who annually paid him to stalk and often bag their trophies for them. He took their money and strapped his deer to their bumpers for the show-off ride down the turnpike.) Living in Italy, however, my Bambi complex became confirmed, as did my sympathy for those little birds who dressed up Cinderella, for Big Bird . . . for Tweety.

A magazine story by Francesco Mezzatesta, one of the most prominent and outspoken of Italian bird-watchers, did nothing to free me from my complexes. He describes the fate of a migrating red-capped shrike that landed exhausted on the deck of a ferry returning him and a group of bird-watchers to Tuscany from the Island of Capraia. Having almost completed the exhausting flight from the Sahara and over the Mediterranean, the tired shrike chanced a free ride, trying to save its life, Mezzatesta explains. Within moments, however, two mocking sailors forced the harmless bird off the deck and back to sea, to rowdy cheers of approval from a group of young Tuscan hunters who also happened to be on board. After the bird disappeared, the hunters turned to making fun of the outraged birders. Other passengers simply looked on in silence. Mezzatesta saw in this tale an allegory, exemplifying not only the unnecessary cruelty of the sailors and the hunters, but the dangerous passivity of observers who are reluctant to speak out against them.

I occasionally read of victories in favor of the birds, referenda limiting hunters—the kinds and numbers of birds they can take, the weapons and equipment they can use—reaffirmations of the 1979 Bern Convention that "forbids the capturing, caging, or selling of the wild birds of Europe," ratified in Italy in 1982. I then read about the police confiscating caged sparrows, mistle thrushes, song thrushes, terns, skylarks, blackbirds, fieldfares, and starlings at the Fiera degli Uccelli. (No wonder those salesmen seemed so edgy as I wandered among the cages.)

I read also of pro-bird societies—the World Wildlife Fund, the Alliance for the Abolition of Hunting, Italia Nostra, Lega Ambiente, Amici della Terra—of nature parks, reserves, refuges, and oases, and of conferences on water pollution and other hazards to the birds, bioregional fiestas in honor of birds, and bird-watching camps, one specifically designed to support the honey buzzard, a raptor from Africa killed in Sicily as a talisman to ensure wives' fidelity.

And I read about LIPU, the Lega Italiana Protezione Uccelli, or Alliance for the Protection of Birds, the largest organization acting exclusively on the birds' behalf. It is LIPU that sponsors the Guardia Venatoria, or Hunting Guard, monitoring hunters in the field and fining them when they break the law. I even read of some enlightened hunters who claim sympathy with the birds, publicly supporting endangered species laws and caring for wounded birds. But I also learned of dogs killed, tires punctured, and cars burned when protectionists stood too firmly in the path of the centuries-old pursuit of wild birds—a national patrimony, the hunters claim.

I turned to the galleries and churches for some relief. Here too was a national patrimony. At the Medici palace I discovered colorful birds in Gozzoli's frescoes, painted in a safe corner, out of danger. At the Uffizi were Bachiacca's tapestries of the months, busy with birds both illustrating the seasons and decorating the borders, and here too was Raphael's charming Madonna del Cardellino, where the Christ child pets a bird being presented to him by Saint John as Mary looks on approvingly.

I learned more of Benvenuto Cellini and of Leonardo da Vinci, said to have captured birds for the pleasure of releasing them. And at Santa Maria Novella I studied Paulo Doni's "Deluge" frescoes, searching for the birds that inspired him to change his name to Uccello, or Bird, in praise of them.

My courage renewed, I finally decided to visit the Florence LIPU office for more up-to-date local information. Here I heard more disheartening statistics, but I was also invited by Sandro Sacchetti, head of the local LIPU chapter, to visit one of the best bird-watching sites around Florence—Osmannoro. This small wetland, made up mostly of reedy marsh, survives precariously within an industrial and commercial zone and too near the only Florentine airport, Peretola. I was surprised to find it there at all, and I certainly would never have come upon it myself, but what surprised me even more was that this was actually a bird hunters' game preserve, complete with shed, lookouts, gun rests, and guards.

On a gently flowery April day that would have cheered Botticelli's *Primavera*, a khaki-clad hunter met us at our car, warmly shook Sandro's hand, and led us through the chain-link gate.

Armed with bird books and binoculars, we passed through a rustic shed, ruffling the dog-eared hunting magazines strewn across a tipsy table. Just outside the shed, snuggled up to a low fence, nested a contented mallard. The juxtapositions were confusing.

At the blind, I rested my elbows on the gun rest to steady my binoculars while Sandro and the hunter competed in identifying over thirty species of birds and translating their names into English for me, among them shoveler, gray heron, greylag goose, Hooper swan, whiskered tern, great white egret, and little ringed plover. Little bitterns, sand martins, and night herons were breeding there. Reed warblers chorused from the grassy periphery. A trim *cavaliere d'Italia*, in its parade black and white, with long red legs for boots, strutted among the ducks and egrets as if inspecting the troops.

Within an hour I identified more Italian birds than I had ever seen before; they were crowded yet fortunate to be at least temporarily safe in this small chain-link enclosure. The hunters and the birders were crowded together too, forced into an uncomfortable alliance against the opposition, those who sought to turn this "duckpond" into another runway for the airport. Like the birds, they didn't have the luxury of not getting along.

As the birds chattered and the observers all grumbled in unison about the eager developers and Florence's ever-widening grasp, planes dipped low to the runway and a lifting helicopter drowned out all other sounds. I lingered at the gun rest, looking across the marsh, across the runway, across the north Florentine flatness. Through the haze, the Duomo, one of humanity's most glorious achievements and one of Italy's most alluring attractions, emerged with imposing clarity. Will the pressure from all sides cause the hunters and the birders to form permanent new alliances? Will necessity make them less combative with one another? Sandro did suggest that with constant vigilance things might get better for the birds, but then he added, "The trouble is, we really don't know how much time we have."

At another site near Peretola, also threatened by industrial expansion, Sandro helped me spot a little grebe and two rare white-winged terns coasting low over the grass in graceful intertwining circles. Sedge warblers, fan-tailed warblers, and white-throated warblers sang from the reeds and scrubby brush on our side of the marsh.

With a random sweep of my binoculars, my heart jumped when I spotted a twiggy tree literally sagging with birds of many shapes and sizes. It was so laden that it could have served as one of those "identitrees" silhouetted in bird guides or painted on dish towels.

But my excitement was ill founded. All these birds were decoys, set strategically to lure their own kind into gun range. As long before at Virgil's deadly Lake Avernus, there wasn't a breathing bird among them.

The River of Grass

The "glades" of Florida's "Everglades" suggests a clear, open, bright space, related to the Anglo-Saxon *glaed*, or "joyful." The intention of the "ever" is certain, an evocation of permanence, reaching from eons past to a timeless future. It's a mellifluous name, with ease and naturalness in its very letters. The name not only is a description, it is an invitation to slow down, even to idle, because in these glades there is ever more time to be had.

To get there, after a January flight from Boston, we drove down Florida's rowdy Route 1, a rude battering of chaotic traffic, burger delights, billboards touting stuffed potatoes, and kiosks for land-grab bargains on the Keys. At the park gates I gave up the steering wheel to Frank, reclined the passenger seat, and fell into a groggy sleep, surrendering to exhaustion and relief. Nothing interrupted the soothing hum of the tires. Nothing needed my attention, and for the few moments I was able to stay awake, I felt grateful.

Almost at the end of the long, flat road to Flamingo on the bay, a road described as "fifty miles of nothing" by more than one critic, I finally resurfaced. The setting sun cast a gauzy green gray haze over everything—or maybe my eyes weren't quite open yet. It didn't seem to matter. We were the only ones on the road. No cars, no signs, no hitchhikers, no animals, no birds demanded our attention. It was a blissful vacancy.

Tired himself now, Frank pulled to the side of the road and closed his eyes. I offered to drive again, but I was happy when he murmured "just a few minutes" and fell asleep. Still half dozing myself, I checked the map for the one road we could possibly be on and looked out the window across the saw grass rippling in the shadowy evening breeze, more like water than grass.

With more attention, I noticed that in one place it was parting like hair under a comb, then closing back up to rejoin the ripples. Idly I followed the path of this parting until, only feet from our car, two adult raccoons emerged, followed by a train of obedient young. They ambled a short way down the shoulder, then disappeared back into the grass, visible only in the neat line that itself disappeared into the deepening shadows.

During my three-day stay in the 'glades, I often experienced this now you see us, now you don't elusiveness. A knobby, lumpish shape in Mrazek Pond was a floating log . . . no, not a log, but one . . . no, three . . . baby alligators. A long strip of tire rubber on the shoulder of the road became, close up, a black snake sunning.

At Taylor Slough I watched another snake ripple the surface of the water then waddle awkwardly onto dry land and up to a low branch, where it spread its silvery wings to dry. Not a snake, an anhinga, kin to the cormorant. The marina fence post in the dark, bending toward the water, was a little green heron on a night hunt. The next green heron turned out to be a fence post. The Everglades plays tricks.

After the headlong collision of the semester's end with the solid demands of the Christmas season, after the December ice storms, and before the second half of the school year where English literature, research papers, and major essayists awaited, this park was an easy place to be. Once we got past the strangely unnerving Santa Clauses beckoning from the rooftops through the highway heat, it was a pleasure to drift with the rippling saw grass. Simply trading my down jacket for a light sweater was a measurable relief.

The Everglades is not fast paced, not showy; it gives the sense that nothing is moving, nothing is going anywhere. Because of its overgrown quality, Marjorie Stoneman Douglas aptly named this place the "river of grass," but this is a slow-moving river, slipping toward the sea at only a quarter of a mile a day.

At bays, we stopped to watch herons standing tall, their legs like tree roots, waiting for the unwary fish much as they do at the pond near my house; but in this glossy, flat expanse, these herons seemed somehow even more still. We watched alligators lounging motionless, possibly waiting for a garfish to swim near, and we watched garfish also waiting—tiny shafts balanced in the still water—their shadows more animated than they. It's fitting that snails are among the major wildlife sightings at the Everglades.

In 1947, after fifty years of fighting, these 1,398,800 acres of grass and water were made into a national park, with President Truman claiming, "We have permanently safeguarded an irreplaceable primitive area." In 1979 the region was made a World Heritage Site by the United Nations, placing it among such earthly wonders as the Galápagos, Mount Everest, and the Serengeti Plain. But still some guidebooks inform, even warn, that the pleasures here are subtle, requiring the visitor to "give to the 'glades something before it gives you anything." That "something" is attention to the smaller, often inconspicuous delights waiting everywhere to be noticed but making no demands. It was perfect for me. I loved the quietness, I loved the strangeness, I loved the puzzles.

I read descriptions of gumbo-limbo trees, mockingly called "tourist trees" because they peel as if sunburned, and then I saw them, ragged and flayed, along the trails. I recognized the strangler figs, wrapped in a death grip around their "host trees," and I found the air plants high among the branches of ancient mahoganies, themselves exotics.

One late afternoon, wandering along a boardwalk among the vines and thick greenery of a hardwood hammock, I first heard and then spotted a bird I had only hoped to see—the white-crowned pigeon. The next day I searched out the striped liguus tree snails glistening on the trunks of tall pines, the whole scene looking more like an illustration for a prehistory textbook than like real life. With less attention, I could easily have missed all these things.

At lunchtime we rowed easily out onto the placid bay and followed the path of a brown pelican breaking the silence of our picnic with headlong dives for fish. On the way back I finally glimpsed my first great white heron, the bird I had once mistakenly identified on a New England bay, but this one was where it should be—a ghostly whiteness hidden deep among the mangrove roots. The Everglades is a place for the ease deprived.

I did see hints of the summer mosquitoes: the netting on the tourist trolleys, the little mosquito-emblazoned Red Cross badges with the message "We gave at Everglades National Park." And I did take notice of the warnings against befriending the alligators. But the winter Everglades forced no challenges that we didn't bring upon ourselves. With no tumbling cascades, no multicolored deserts, no gigantic trees, no erupting geysers, no grand canyons, it was not spectacular. And I was glad.

It was during my relaxing time-outs from my resting that I discovered an irony in this absence of grandeur. Facing the long lawn at Flamingo, looking out to the pelicans diving into the bay, I read that this very plainness made the task of preserving the Everglades all the more difficult. It was a long struggle to convince others to preserve this mosquito-infested, storm-blasted, inhospitable alligator pool, and the struggle was not entirely successful.

President Truman had designated the area a national park, and others had added their voices to its protection, but preservation, though continuing, is still not sure. Apprehensive, I read of the threats to the "ever" of the Everglades. From the north comes an irregular, unreliable water supply; from the south come tropical storms, tearing up mangrove trees and toppling mahoganies; from the west come speculators and sports boaters seeking access to the swamplands; from the east come metropolitan Miami and the demands of the farmers. From below salt water invades the fresh groundwater, and from above the air rains pollution. To some it may be a national treasure, competing with the glories of Everest, but to others it is a sodden tract of wasted real estate.

I then read tales of plenty from the past, like Audubon's description of the area as a bird-watcher's Eden and the account by eighteenth-century botanist William Bartram, who reported that it was possible to walk across an Everglades river on the backs of alligators, should the hiker be so inclined. Marjorie Stoneman Douglas sang of a rich, stagey abundance where "over all this thick jungle region climbed and hung down in moving green curtains the heart-shaped leaves of moonvines," but she also described a more current Everglades as an "awful mess," a place threatened with extinction.

The more I read about the complex, and sometimes conflicting, efforts to preserve the place, the more I compared the scene before me with the abundance of the past, the more my ease became weighted with anxiety.

Listening through the silence for the call of a limpkin, counting the individuals in the flock of skimmers all turned to the west into the sun, peering through the darkness for a panther on the night trail, I was too easily haunted by visions of those eerie, beckoning Santas just outside the park gates. Santa goes a-marketing, I thought, and I bet he would love to build a mall right about here. I then recited to myself one of those familiar English-major poems by Wordsworth:

> *The world is too much with us, late and soon,*
> *Getting and spending, we lay waste our powers*
> *Little we see in nature that is ours,*
> *A sordid boon . . .*

It was all too easy to update and broaden Wordsworth's message. Little did he know; he never laid eyes on Route 1.

There I was, meandering down Snake Bight Trail, a luxuriant wooded walk with curiosities around every corner, but still harking back to classroom recitations, with accompanying explications. I smiled to myself when I recalled the many occasions at my desk with the books demanding immediate attention—"Isn't it time you got us read?"—when I longed for an escape down any trail. Now, on this trail, I was reverting to the pithy poetic messages of early nineteenth-century England.

I suppose it's not surprising that the literature I've been teaching for years would come to mind. After all, it often includes exhortations to appreciate the natural world, probably one of the main reasons I was there on that trail at all. It was writers like Wordsworth who sent me off on this lifelong walk in the first place. Sitting alone on an abandoned dock at the edge of the bay and watching the flashing shifts and turns of a large flock of dunlins, I reminded myself of what it was that drew me to literature and then to the birds. It was at least partly the quiet, as I was experiencing it at that moment, the chance to be silent and to appreciate messages from places other than my own life's sources. It was the unobtrusive, chosen pleasures. It was the chance to feel, in a way so seductively described by Yeats:

> *we can make our minds so like still water that beings gather about us that they may see, it may be, their own images, and so live for a moment with a clearer, perhaps even with a fiercer life because of our quiet.*

It was the search for this "fiercer life" that sent me off to the libraries and down the trails through the woods. It's the rewards of quietness that I always hope my own students will come to love.

But it's not so easy now, I thought. The 'glades certainly are threatened by forces from all sides, but I sometimes worry that the literature too may be threatened not only by our devotion to getting and spending but also by the "sordid boons" of the profession that claims it. Appreciating literature nowadays seems too often an effort to keep the beckoning Santas of academe from gesturing too frantically, distracting us from the pleasures on the page. It's sometimes hard to keep the poetry in mind what with the wrangling committees, the inputs, the throughputs, the outcomes, the surveys, the documents, the questionnaires, the assessments, and especially the curriculum disputes where each new covenant wages war against this or that power group. Then there are the latest efforts to show us the error of our outworn ways.

Add to all this the further clutter of cyber-spaced-out lingo: the interfaces, webs, browsers, homepages, and hypertexts; the effortless, often mindless typing that reaches the entire world; and the sometimes tone-deaf computer talk translated in a whole new subgenre of books written specifically for slow movers, math phobics, and downright dummies. Sometimes Wordsworth's sordid boon seems bought and paid for.

I knew that Wordsworth's friend Charles Lamb had refused an invitation to the poet's house in the Lake District by declaring, "Separate from the pleasure of your company, I don't much care if I never see a mountain in my life," but he was an eccentric. I couldn't help wondering, though, if Wordsworth himself could now make as much time for those sunsets fading in the west.

And then I thought of Thoreau's timely comment on the laying of the Atlantic Cable: "We are eager to tunnel under the Atlantic and bring the old world some weeks nearer to the new; but perchance the first news that will leak through into the broad, flapping American ear will be that the Princess Adelaide has the whooping cough." I was sure that the irony of the literary profession's contributions to the current din, more than ever transoceanic, would not be lost on Thoreau, nor would he hesitate to point out that the business of literature may all too easily become a distraction from the real life before our eyes. Sometimes there is just too much busyness, too much noise, too much concern for the instrument that brings us news of Princess Adelaide.

On the way out of the 'glades, heading to the airport and back to the classroom, we stopped for one last look at tiny Mrazek Pond. Alligators, definitely alligators, rested loglike in the sun, and a snowy egret set off across the water. Stretching out long white wings and letting his legs dangle, he dragged his bright yellow feet across the surface. Back and forth he moved, toward the viny greenery and then to the small rooty patch from which he had lifted off. I had never seen a bird behave quite this way before. I didn't know what he was doing, and at that point I didn't really care. I simply enjoyed watching his whiteness pass, backlit by the sun, the pond glittering, the splashing softly ruffling the silence. I wanted that moment to last forever.

With this visit it became even clearer to me that at least part of my job is to shut down the clamor long enough for my students to make their own minds more like Yeats's "still water," open to the joys that flourish only in peace and quiet.

Maybe, if the writers themselves aren't drowned out by contention, they will help these students to sort out the messages, to recognize what is worth saving, to ask Santa to put his hand down for a while, maybe to take him for a walk. Maybe, if they listen carefully enough, they'll be around to protect places like the Everglades and to prevent the "Nevermore!" of Poe's ominous raven from becoming the last word.

Why Watch a Bird?

Before an early Monday class, as I was twittering on with a student about weekend bird-watching delights, one of her more earthbound classmates piped up, "Why *watch* a bird? I can see *eating* 'em, but just going out and watching? No way!"

To this I responded with a devastating, "Well . . . ah . . . well . . . there are lots of reasons," adding firmly, "*lots* of them," thus lending emphasis to my total lack of content.

The hour hand of the clock and the need to get on with major eighteenth-century essayists (which I *can* list) rescued me from filling in the blanks.

As so often happens, I thought later of what I might have said.

First of all, I don't know why other people watch birds. But I do now have some thoughts about why *I* do.

For one thing, I find watching birds relaxing, a temporary and often brief escape from the speed of my life where I find myself yearning for double time, a life running alongside the one I'm living, just so I can get everything done. Birdwatchers must learn how to wait, to wait for the redstart, heard but not yet seen;

to wait for the shearwater to drift close enough for identification as a "Manx"; to wait for a bald eagle to finish lunch.

When I allow myself the time, I relax simply watching birds being birds—following the cardinal from feeding ground to nesting site, and back, and forth, and back, or witnessing the kingbird's spirited defense of his airspace against a crow. Nope, I'm not just idly lolling under this fir tree, I'm waiting for the great horned owl to return to his spring branch—one of these days.

I also enjoy the discovery in bird-watching. I enjoy naming my daily next-tree neighbors and the rare exotics in trees far from home. I think of that first *named* black-capped chickadee, a bird I probably tripped over as a child but never really saw, and I still feel the pleasure of making the matchup in my guide. I also remember a ridiculous early debate with my husband about whether a sandpiper strolling along the seashore should be labeled "solitary" because it was alone or "spotted" because we had seen it. When we turned to the more reliable field marks in our guide, we happily came up with an indisputable diagnosis of spotted.

I identified my first red-winged blackbird by trilling an imitation of the call described in my guide and finally matching it to the *tee-err* and *konk-la-ree* drifting from a nearby swamp. And by sight and sound, I named some of those more elusive birds winging by in Florida, in Italy, in Kenya. Yes, the naïve thrill of recognizing which bird is which declines with the efficiency of the watcher, but the pleasure of knowing at least some of them by name carries on, making the world more familiar, sometimes more comfortable.

I feel a kind of rightness when the snowy owls return to their icy lookouts and I return to find them. I like the predictability of the May warblers that festoon the trees at the local cemetery. I watch for the osprey setting up housekeeping on her ocean-blasted platform, for the woodcock soaring over the brushy field in his spring courtship dance, and for the hundreds of migrating hawks spiraling over the September mountain.

In fact, I pace my own life to a sort of insistent rhythm, and birds enhance my awareness of it. Almost every September of my life, I've set off to school, as a student and then as a teacher. The first working day after Labor Day is my real annual beginning, a greater shift of spirits than the champagne, tooters, and forced frolic of the New Year. With some relief, I abandon the self-guided distractions of summer, and head up the road to students, syllabi, examinations, corrections, recommendations, committees, and due-dates until May. Like the birds, I migrate to a new life in autumn.

I like the rhythms of this schedule; they seem in harmony with larger, more universal rhythms, with those that drive the planet. As I pack up for my commute, I look for signs that nature is packing with me. The chill in the morning air hints of snowstorms, the first red maple begins to turn, the flowers take on tough autumnal tones, and the geese at the pond get restless and noisy again. Some years, the birds and I move in a kind of synchronized passing. As I turn the car north to school, they set off south noisily over my head, toward their new seasons elsewhere.

At this time of year, birds remind me that major things are happening with or without me, that my place is within a system much larger than my own.

Maybe it was this recognition that led me to another one— that birds have real lessons to teach. Birds warn us to be careful. It's impossible to watch them for long without becoming aware of the fluctuations in their total numbers, without reading about the many threats to their survival.

It's impossible to stand before the grim dodo display case at the Oxford University Museum, or to see the grainy black-and-white photograph of the last passenger pigeon at the Cincinnati Zoo, or to visit the last small community of whooping cranes at their Aransas National Park wintering site in Texas without facing what extinction really means, without realizing we could lose the birds that are still with us.

As so many have already pointed out, this awareness of how the birds are doing may indeed help us keep things in perspective. But it may also be a cause for anxiety, even fright, as we are also reminded of what might happen to us if we don't remember where we all fit. It may not be only the caged canaries in the mine shafts that have toxic warnings to deliver.

But bird-watching may also offer encouragement about things that are still going right. At Machias Seal Island off the coast of Maine, for example, families of puffins seem to pose for pictures; at Cap Sizun in Brittany, kittiwakes chorus by the thousands, and near Skellig Michael off the coast of Ireland, grandstands of gannets nest in tiers on the rocky cliffs. Then there are the birds that have conquered the deadly gases of Lake Avernus, and stock the bird paradise of Kenya's Lake Nakuru. Fears may linger, but such evidence of plenty does temper despair.

It isn't necessary for me to go so far for signs of hope, though. Every year migrants return to my yard and to my pond. Every year they flock to the cemetery in Cambridge, Massachusetts. Birds often come my way, like that Ross's gull many years ago or that snowy owl resting sunlit in the wind as if in an avian fashion show. Near an ornamental pool in a garden one evening, I looked up a tree trunk only to see it looking back at me. A small hole in the tree framed a tiny screech owl face on unblinking alert, a picture of concentration. Sometimes the birds are closer than we think.

And then there was my encounter, many years after my first, with a black-capped chickadee. As I walked a trail in the deep woods, the bird landed on a rhododendron bush beside me, leaned in my direction, and tilted its head expectantly, seeming to want something. So I put my finger out for a perch, an offer it took immediately, settling there for a full minute, nibbling gently at my fingernail, then fluttering back to the bush. I had read of a crow marching across a sleeper's pillow, and of a blue jay tapping at a windowpane for breakfast, and I knew that others handle wild birds daily—banding, mist-netting, protecting—but this was the closest the wild had come to me, a meeting I still like to recall.

Thinking over the answers I didn't give that student, I came up with other reasons too that birds are worth watching. They are, after all, often beautiful—the flashy scarlet of the tanager high in a tree, the great blue heron lifting off with huge wing thrusts and soaring over my car on the backed-up highway, the fiery spring goldfinch balancing on the hanging feeder, the familiar robin pulling a worm from the morning lawn.

Not man-made, they take us beyond ourselves, stirring imagination, inspiring us to metaphor, like Thoreau's vireo that seems more than ready to accept the responsibility:

> *Upon the lofty elm tree sprays*
> *The vireo rings the changes sweet.*
> *During the trivial summer days,*
> *Striving to lift our thoughts above the street.*

My pleasure in both the real birds and the literary ones arises from the same source. My students aren't at all surprised if I report on the kestrel I watched on the weekend before I get around to discussing Gerard Manley Hopkins's "The Windhover."

And the bird-watchers themselves, both professional and amateur, are an inspiration. Take, for example, those students of migration who have captured and banded millions of birds, put collars on Canada geese, dyed knots' red breasts orange, traced bird paths across the face of the moon, followed routes on radar, tracked flocks with telescopes and satellites, suspended birds in boxes attached to balloons, realigned the heavens under planetarium skies, and who might have, like Professor Charles Walcott, a student of homing pigeons, spent "several thousand hours flying all over New England after radio-equipped pigeons."

I like knowing that while I'm in class trying to explain Shelley's skylark, these watchers are out there tracking down the real ones.

And in the fields where I walk, the more casual bird-watchers are also a pleasing flock. Many of the most remarkable birds I've seen were pointed out to me by a watcher with a better eye than mine. Both professional and amateur, they're the ones who pay attention to what birds are where; they're the ones who name them, count them, keep track of them. They're the ones who worry daily about how the birds are doing and who care what message Thoreau's vireo might have for us.

The next time someone asks why I spend so much time looking at birds, I'll be a little faster with a response. But I can see that I'll be accumulating many more years of answers before *this* list is complete.

Acknowledgments

I would like to express my gratitude to many people—Tom McCarthy, D. A. Oliver, and Scott Kirkman of Ragged Mountain Press; the editors of various journals who helped me greatly along the way, especially David Wiegand, formerly of the *Cambridge Chronicle;* John Mitchell of *Sanctuary*, and Tim Gallagher of *Living Bird;* the many bird-watchers, both professional and amateur, who took the trouble to guide me across unfamiliar terrain; literature teachers too numerous to name; colleagues and friends, especially Ellen Vellela and Alicia Nitecki; and my family, so much a part of all that is explored here—my son, Geoff, my daughter, Julia, and my husband, Frank Blessington, my first reader and most helpful critic. I would finally like to acknowledge the inspiration of my many students at Salem State College—listeners, readers, writers, and friends over the years.

Versions of the following essays have been previously published: "Watching the Watchers" (*Sanctuary*), "A Blessing for a Lifetime" (*WildBird*), "An Owl or Not an Owl?" (*Cambridge Chronicle*), "Gilbert White's Selborne" (*The Christian Science Monitor*), "With the

Twitchers in England" (*WildBird*), "Reading John o' Words Again" (*Living Bird*), "La Colombina, Non È Andata Bene!" (*Boston Globe*), "Venice: A City on the Wing" (*Boston Globe*), "The Tune in the Tree" (*Sanctuary*), "Life-Listing in Kenya" (*Boston Globe*), "Waiting for an Eagle" (*Appalachia Bulletin*), "Watched by the Birds in India" (*Snowy Egret*), "Coming Back to Capistrano" (*Off Main Street*), "The Attractions of Ukpik" (*Sanctuary*), "Birdwatching . . . in Italy?" (*Living Bird*),"The River of Grass" (*Sextant*), "Why Watch a Bird?" (*Christian Science Monitor*).

Verse by Seamus Heaney on page 135 quoted from "St. Kevin and the Blackbird," in *Opened Ground: Selected Poems 1966–1996*, by Seamus Heaney (Farrar, Straus & Giroux, 1998). Reprinted with permission.

Verse on page 127 quoted from *Tales from the Igloo*, by Maurice Metayer. Copyright © 1977 by Maurice Metayer. Reprinted by permission of St. Martin's Press, Incorporated.

About the Author

Ann Taylor, a professor of English at Salem State College in Salem, Massachusetts, writes personal essays on a variety of subjects, especially travel and bird-watching. Her essays have appeared in publications such as the *Boston Globe*, the *Christian Science Monitor*, and Massachusetts Audubon's *Sanctuary*, among others. She has read an essay on National Public Radio on why she watches birds and published articles on literature and on writing and two textbooks, *Short Model Essays* and *Shaping the Short Essay*. She lives in Woburn, Massachusetts, with her husband, Francis Blessington, and their two children, Geoffrey and Julia.

"A collection of delightfully personal reflections on a wide variety of experiences as an amateur bird watcher, respectful of the reality at hand yet mindful of the feeling and meaning it arouses in the observer."

—Leonard Lutwack, author of *Birds in Literature*

"Taylor displays enviable promise as an essayist, possessing clarity and a facility with both dark and comic experiences. Be thankful for the serendipities she captures, luminous instants like a trill heard in the silent snowy woods."

—*Kirkus Reviews*

"It is literature that lures Tayor into bird-watching, a comfortable, refreshing approach."

—*Publishers Weekly*

Printed in the United States
24565LVS00006B/10